The Beginner's Guide to Chakras

Unlock Your Full Potential with Easy Chakra Balancing Methods

Natasha Parker BSc (Hons) Psych

Table of Contents

Introduction ... 3
Understanding the Chakra System ... 8
The Root Chakra: Foundation and Stability ... 21
   Signs of a Balanced vs. Imbalanced Root Chakra ... 22
   Grounding Exercises and Techniques to Connect with the Earth ... 25
   Nutritional Support for Root Chakra Health ... 28
The Sacral Chakra: Creativity and Emotion ... 32
   Emotional Indicators of Sacral Chakra Imbalance ... 33
   Creative Pursuits to Stimulate Sacral Chakra Energy ... 37
   Healing Through Sensory Experiences and Activities ... 40
The Solar Plexus Chakra: Personal Power ... 46
   Impact of Personal Power on Decision-Making and Willpower ... 47
   Breathing Techniques to Activate the Solar Plexus ... 51
   Affirmations to Boost Self-Worth and Confidence ... 54
The Heart Chakra: Love and Connection ... 60
   Balancing Giving and Receiving in Personal Relationships ... 61
   Practices for Cultivating Kindness and Empathy ... 64
   Relationships Between Heart Chakra and Forgiveness ... 66
The Throat Chakra: Expression and Communication ... 72
   Techniques to Improve Vocal Expression and Authenticity ... 73

- Listening Skills as Part of Healthy Throat Chakra Activity ... 76
- Impact of Honest Communication on Personal Growth ... 78
- The Third Eye Chakra: Intuition and Insight ... 84
  - Meditation Practices to Enhance Intuitive Capabilities ... 85
  - Decoding Dreams and Symbols in Third Eye Development ... 88
  - Releasing Negative Thoughts to Clear Mental Clutter ... 92
  - Bringing It All Together ... 96
- The Crown Chakra: Spirituality and Enlightenment ... 99
  - Connecting with Universal Consciousness through Prayer and Meditation ... 100
  - Balancing Ego with Higher Consciousness ... 103
  - Integrating Chakra Work into Daily Life for Sustained Spiritual Growth ... 107
  - Final Insights ... 111
- Conclusion ... 114
- References ... 120

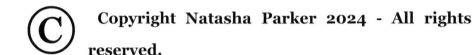 Copyright Natasha Parker 2024 - All rights reserved.

The content within this book may not be reproduced, duplicated or transmitted without direct written permission from the author or the publisher.

Under no circumstances will any blame or legal responsibility be held against the publisher, or author, for any damages, reparation, or monetary loss due to the information contained within this book. Either directly or indirectly. You are responsible for your own choices, actions, and results.

Legal Notice:

This book is copyright protected. This book is only for personal use. You cannot amend, distribute, sell, use, quote or paraphrase any part, of the content within this book, without the consent of the author or publisher.

Disclaimer Notice:

Please note the information contained within this document is for educational and entertainment purposes only. All effort has been expended to present accurate, up-to-date, and reliable, complete information. No warranties of any kind are declared or implied. Readers acknowledge that the author is not engaging in the rendering of legal, financial, medical or professional advice. The content within this book has been derived from various sources. Please consult a licensed professional before attempting any techniques outlined in this book.

By reading this document, the reader agrees that under no circumstances is the author responsible for any losses, direct or indirect, which are incurred as a result of the use of the information contained within this document, including, but not limited to, — errors, omissions, or inaccuracies.

Introduction

Have you ever felt overwhelmingly anxious or inexplicably joyful? What if the key to understanding these emotions lies within the unseen energy centers of your body—your chakras? Imagine having a tool that not only helps you make sense of these feelings but also empowers you to transform them for a healthier, more balanced life. Welcome to the fascinating world of chakra healing—a journey into understanding and tuning the vital energy centers that shape every part of you.

For centuries, cultures around the world have tapped into the power of chakras, recognizing their profound impact on our mind, body, and spirit. Originating from ancient Eastern traditions, chakras are not just mystical concepts reserved for yogis and healers. Rather, they represent the essential energy pathways that influence all dimensions of our well-being. Picture them as colorful wheels spinning within you, each responsible for different aspects of who you are and how you interact with the world. Each chakra governs specific areas of your life, affecting physical health, emotional stability, and spiritual growth.

In today's fast-paced, high-stress society, many people experience feelings of disconnection and imbalance. The pressures of modern life often leave us feeling out of sync with ourselves and others, leading to stress, anxiety, and a range of other challenges. But imagine if there was a way to amplify your energy, clear emotional blockages, and reconnect with your deeper self. Chakra healing offers this transformative potential. By becoming aware of your chakras and learning how to nurture them, you embark on a journey of personal growth and self-discovery, where you can unlock hidden potentials and bring greater harmony into your everyday life.

This book is your guide through this enlightening path. Over the following chapters, we'll delve into the mysteries and wonders of each of the seven major chakras. These aren't mere theoretical discussions; rather, you'll be introduced to practical insights and actionable techniques designed to help you engage actively with your energy system. We'll explore the unique functions of each chakra, signs of imbalance, and straightforward methods to bring them back into alignment.

You don't need any previous knowledge or special equipment to begin this journey. All you require is an open mind and a willingness to explore new dimensions of yourself. Whether you aim to enhance your physical vitality, achieve emotional equilibrium, or embark on a spiritual journey, understanding and working with your chakras can invigorate and illuminate your life's path.

We'll start with the Root Chakra, the foundation of your energetic being, linked to your sense of safety and groundedness. We'll learn how connecting with this chakra can provide stability and security in all aspects of life. Moving upwards, we will venture into the Sacral Chakra, which influences creativity and relationships, guiding you to embrace change and passion.

As we continue our exploration, the Solar Plexus Chakra awaits, where personal power and self-esteem reside. Here, you will find ways to cultivate confidence and assert your rightful place in the world. Rising further, the Heart Chakra opens the doors to love and compassion, teaching ways to give and receive affection honestly and openly.

The Throat Chakra will encourage you to speak your truth and express yourself authentically. It's here that you'll discover the keys to better communication and the courage to stand up for what you believe.

Through to the Third Eye Chakra, you'll gain insight into intuition and foresight, learning to trust your inner wisdom to make informed decisions. Finally, at the crown sits the Crown Chakra, connecting us to higher consciousness and spiritual enlightenment, inviting you to explore broader existential questions and your place in the universe.

By the end of this book, you'll have gained not only knowledge but also hands-on experience in chakra healing practices. You'll have tools at your disposal, like meditations, exercises, and lifestyle adjustments, to apply these insights in real-life scenarios. You'll be equipped to maintain balance and find peace even amid chaos, leading to a richer, more fulfilled life.

Are you ready to take the first step on this transformative journey? Embrace the possibility of living at your highest potential by exploring the vibrant spectrum of your chakra system. Turn the page, and let's embark on this adventure together, unlocking energies that can transform your world from within. Your life is about to become a canvas of colors and vibrations you never knew existed. Discover the healer within by harnessing the power of your chakras, and see how this ancient wisdom can profoundly impact your modern life.

Understanding the Chakra System

Exploring the chakra system is like getting to know an unseen map of your body's energy highways. These chakras, thought of as spinning wheels of energy, have been present in ancient philosophies and continue to intrigue people today. Their historical roots are deep, originating from Hindu texts that have painted them as integral to spiritual practices across centuries. They're not just confined to one culture or tradition; these energy centers have been embraced by various spiritual beliefs, including Buddhism, which uses them as focal points for meditation and self-awareness. Each tradition adds its flavor, integrating chakras into broader systems of health and spirituality. The idea of having such energy hubs within us can spark curiosity and prompt a journey toward better understanding how they influence our lives.

From their inception in ancient Hindu scriptures to their adaptation in Buddhist practices, you'll discover how these concepts have been shaped and molded through time, resonating with many philosophies. You'll also explore how these ideas have jumped across continents, morphing along the way to become part of Western holistic practices. We'll look at how each of these chakras connects with aspects of life, influencing everything from emotional balance to spiritual growth. As you turn the pages, get ready to see how a legacy that spans thousands of years continues to influence wellness approaches globally, offering insights that might just change the way you perceive your own well-being.

Historical Origins and Influences

Chakras are an ancient concept with deep roots in Hinduism, where they are seen as vital energy centers within the body. The idea of chakras dates back thousands of years and is documented in ancient Indian texts like the Vedas. These texts form the foundation of many spiritual practices, making chakras central to understanding the life force in humans. According to these traditions, each chakra corresponds to a specific aspect of human experience and spiritual potential. The flow of energy through these chakras is believed to affect one's physical, emotional, and spiritual health.

The seven main chakras in traditional Hindu belief are the Root Chakra, Sacral Chakra, Solar Plexus Chakra, Heart Chakra, Throat Chakra, Third Eye Chakra, and Crown Chakra. Each of these chakras plays a distinct role in maintaining balance and harmony within the individual, symbolizing levels of consciousness from the material to the divine.

Buddhism has adopted and adapted the concept of chakras into its teachings, particularly emphasizing their role in meditation and self-awareness. Chakras in Buddhism might be fewer in number but are deeply integrated into practices aimed at enhancing mindfulness. Through meditation, practitioners focus on these energy centers to cultivate a heightened state of presence and introspection. This practice aids individuals in developing a deeper connection with their thoughts and emotions, thereby enhancing their ability to navigate life's challenges with greater clarity and peace.

In Buddhism, the integration of chakras goes beyond personal health; it serves a spiritual purpose. By focusing on these energy points, practitioners work towards achieving higher states of consciousness, leading them closer to enlightenment—a core goal in Buddhist practice. This approach underscores the essential function of chakras in fostering not only physical wellbeing but also spiritual growth.

Interestingly, the influence of chakras has transcended Eastern philosophies and found resonance in Western holistic wellness and spirituality. In the West, chakras have been incorporated into various alternative therapies aimed at promoting balance and healing. This global adaptation highlights how versatile and enduring the concept of chakras has become, evolving to fit culturally diverse understandings of health and spirituality. Western approaches often meld these ancient ideas with new interpretations, creating a tapestry of practices that range from yoga and meditation to modern energy healing techniques.

The West's interest in chakras gained momentum during the 20th century, largely due to the rising popularity of alternative spiritual movements. These movements were characterized by an openness to Eastern philosophies and a desire to integrate them into a more holistic view of health. As part of this cultural exchange, chakras became linked with various elements such as colors, crystals, and astrological signs, reflecting a growing interest in integrating spiritual beliefs with everyday wellness practices.

Moreover, practices like yoga and meditation, which focus heavily on balancing chakras, have become mainstream in Western health culture. Yoga, for instance, uses postures, breathing exercises, and meditation to support the flow of energy through the chakras, aiming to restore harmony and reduce stress. Similarly, meditation practices encourage individuals to visualize and align their chakras, fostering a sense of calm and well-being.

Also, Reiki, an energy healing practice from Japan, often incorporates chakra work into its sessions, using the energy centers as focal points for healing and relaxation. Practitioners believe that directing energy through the chakras can promote mental and emotional health by addressing imbalances or blockages.

Despite the widespread use of chakras in wellness practices, Western science has been cautious in embracing these concepts fully. While scientific evidence directly linking chakras to physical health improvements remains limited, the psychological benefits of practices associated with chakra balancing, such as reducing anxiety and stress, are more widely acknowledged. Many people report feeling more centered and calm after engaging in activities aimed at balancing their chakras, pointing to the potential value of these practices in fostering well-being.

Chakras' adaptability across different cultures illustrates their continued relevance in contemporary society. Whether viewed as metaphysical constructs or psychological tools, they offer multiple paths to understanding the human experience. They encourage exploration of the self from both an inner perspective, through meditation and mindfulness, and a broader one, by recognizing their historical significance and ongoing evolution.

Basic Functions of the Chakras

In the intricate tapestry of human energy systems, the chakra system stands out as a vibrant spectrum of colors and sensations that weave through our physical and emotional experiences. At the core of this system lie seven main chakras, each with its own unique characteristics and roles, playing an integral part in our holistic well-being.

First, let's delve into the Root Chakra, known as Muladhara. This chakra is located at the base of the spine and is associated with the color red. It serves as our energetic foundation, crucial for grounding and survival. The Root Chakra anchors us to the earth, providing stability and security. Emotionally, it influences our feelings of safety and trust, acting as the bedrock for our mental calmness. When this chakra is balanced, we feel secure in our surroundings; when unbalanced, it can lead to anxiety and fear (Stelter, 2016). For instance, practices such as grounding exercises or mindful walking can help maintain balance, ensuring that we are firmly rooted in both body and psyche.

Moving upward, we encounter the Solar Plexus Chakra, or Manipura, nestled around the navel and radiating the bright warmth of yellow. This chakra governs personal power and self-esteem. It resonates with our capacity to make decisions and assert our will. Like a sun in our belly, it fuels our confidence and determination, allowing us to navigate life with purpose and clarity. When the Solar Plexus Chakra is aligned, we experience heightened self-assurance and a robust sense of identity, making it easier to pursue ambitions without hesitation. Conversely, imbalances here may manifest as a lack of confidence or difficulty in setting boundaries. It's akin to having a sun dimmed by clouds, complicating our path forward.

As we explore further up the chakra ladder, the Heart Chakra, Anahata, introduces itself at the center of our chest with soothing waves of green. Known for its connection to love and compassion, it bridges the spiritual and earthly realms, uniting us with others and the universe at large. Imagine this chakra as a lush garden where emotions like kindness and empathy blossom, nourishing relationships and promoting harmony. When open and vibrant, the Heart Chakra encourages unconditional love and forgiveness. A person with a balanced heart chakra is generous and empathetic, capable of profound connection with others. On the other hand, blockages might trigger feelings of loneliness or resentment, like a wilted garden yearning for care and light.

Nearer our crown lies the Third Eye Chakra, or Ajna, resting subtly between our eyebrows and shining with indigo hues. This chakra sharpens intuition and enhances perception, acting as a gateway to deeper understanding and insight. It is akin to having an internal compass, guiding us toward wisdom and clarity of thought. By fostering a connection with our inner vision, the Third Eye Chakra helps spur personal growth and self-realization. An open Third Eye Chakra allows us to see beyond the superficial, offering perspectives that transcend ordinary sight—seeing things "as they are." When obstructed, however, one may struggle with confusion or lack of foresight, as though trying to navigate through fog.

Understanding these chakras illuminates how profoundly interconnected they are with our physical and psychological states. The root, solar plexus, heart, and third eye play pivotal roles not only individually but also in how they harmonize to influence our overall energetic equilibrium. Their health is not just about spiritual alignment, but about maintaining the symphony of energies that sustain our vitality and drive.

The exploration of chakras doesn't end here. It opens doors to considering how integrating their knowledge into everyday practice can promote healing and enhance life quality. Whether through meditation, breathing exercises, or visualization techniques, nurturing these energetic centers can unlock pathways to greater wellness (Arohan Yoga, 2019). As we become more attuned to the ebb and flow of our energies, the language of chakras becomes less of a mystery and more of a guiding tool in our pursuit of holistic health.

Chakras' Role in Energy Flow and Balance

Chakras serve as vital junctions within the human energy system, acting like wheels that facilitate the flow of life energy—called prana or chi—throughout the body. These energy centers are essential for maintaining both physical and energetic health. When chakras function properly, they ensure the smooth movement of this vital energy, contributing to a harmonious state where the mind, body, and spirit work together seamlessly.

Understanding how chakras manage this energy is pivotal. Imagine them as hubs that receive, process, and transmit prana throughout various parts of your being. They connect with different aspects of our physiology and emotions, influencing everything from mood to physical stamina. For instance, when the chakras are open and balanced, individuals often experience an overall sense of well-being, clarity, and heightened energy levels. However, even slight disruptions in these energy centers can throw off this balance, leading to issues that might manifest emotionally, like anxiety or lack of focus, or physically, such as persistent fatigue.

It's not uncommon for chakras to become blocked or unbalanced due to stress, trauma, or negative habits. This blockage impedes the natural flow of energy, creating pockets of stagnation which can lead to various ailments and discomforts. Identifying these disruptions can guide individuals towards areas that may need healing attention or lifestyle adjustments. Often, people might feel stuck, reactive, or overly stressed without realizing it's an imbalance in their chakra system contributing to these experiences.

Incorporating practices to maintain and restore chakra balance can be immensely beneficial and is relatively straightforward. Yoga and meditation stand out as powerful methods for realigning these centers. Whether it's through meditative exercises aiming at mindfulness or specific yoga postures designed to open up the energy pathways, consistent practice aids in clearing blockages. Another technique is visualization, where one imagines each chakra glowing brightly, spinning freely, helping to mentally reinforce their opening and flow.

Moreover, the benefits of balanced chakras extend into daily life far more than what might initially meet the eye. Regularly engaging in activities that nurture these energy centers can translate to lowered stress levels, improved emotional resilience, and enhanced focus in everyday tasks. The equilibrium achieved through these practices contributes to reducing feelings of overwhelm and cultivating a more serene approach to life's challenges.

For those seeking to integrate chakra balancing into their routines, starting simple is key. Setting aside a few minutes each day for meditation or incorporating yoga sessions multiple times a week can make a notable difference. Even small rituals like deep breathing exercises while visualizing energy moving harmoniously through your chakras can promote substantial shifts in energy balance. These practices serve not only as a means to heal but also as preventative measures to maintain a smoothly functioning energy system.

Additionally, understanding and working with energy flow offers a unique insight into personal health. It empowers individuals to take charge of their wellness journey, transforming the way they relate to their own bodies. Instead of reacting to symptoms, engaging in chakra practices is about addressing the root of an issue through gentle, mindful awareness and proactive care.

Exploring the role of chakras in facilitating energy within us highlights a fascinating intersection between ancient wisdom and modern holistic approaches to health. This understanding encourages a more nuanced perspective on how interconnected we are within ourselves, reminding us of the importance of treating body, mind, and spirit as a cohesive whole.

Summary and Reflections

Throughout this chapter, we've journeyed through the fascinating world of chakras, tracing their origins back to ancient Hindu and Buddhist traditions. These energy centers have been revered for thousands of years, seen not just as mystical constructs but as vital parts of our human experience. The historical context enriches our understanding, showing us how chakras are believed to affect every facet of life—from grounding us to the earth with the Root Chakra to elevating our consciousness through the Crown Chakra. It's intriguing to see how each chakra plays a distinctive role in balancing physical, emotional, and spiritual aspects of life, guiding us toward greater harmony.

In today's modern context, the appeal of chakras has transcended cultures, blending into Western wellness practices where they continue to captivate those seeking holistic health. We've explored how these age-old concepts from Eastern philosophies find new life in alternative therapies geared towards personal well-being. Whether you're practicing yoga, diving into meditation, or simply visualizing these vibrant energy centers, integrating even small chakra-focused rituals can offer profound benefits. As we wrap up this exploration, it becomes clear that chakras serve as powerful gateways into understanding ourselves better, acting as timeless tools to navigate both inner and outer worlds.

The Root Chakra: Foundation and Stability

Understanding the root chakra is like finding the key to your most fundamental sense of well-being. This energy center, often described as the Muladhara, anchors us in the present, providing a base for the experiences and challenges that life throws our way. Picture it as the roots of a tree, deeply connected to the earth, supporting the trunk and branches that represent the rest of your energetic being. It's fascinating how this chakra can influence our feelings of security and stability, acting as an energetic foundation upon which everything else builds. The idea of exploring something so intrinsic, yet sometimes unnoticed, offers both intrigue and promise.

Signs of a Balanced vs. Imbalanced Root Chakra

Recognizing the signs of a balanced or an imbalanced root chakra is an essential step towards achieving personal stability and security. The root chakra, or Muladhara, sits at the base of the spine and represents the foundation upon which our physical and emotional well-being rests. A balanced root chakra provides a solid ground for resilience and vibrant energy, and it manifests physically through a healthy body. When this energy center is in harmony, you experience a deep-rooted sense of safety and are more emotionally stable.

When your root chakra is balanced, you'll often feel grounded and connected to both yourself and your environment. This sense of grounding brings about a feeling of being present and engaged in life. You find it easier to focus and manage day-to-day stressors with a calm mind. With emotional stability comes the ability to face challenges without overwhelming fear or anxiety. Your relationships may flourish as you develop trust in others and in your surroundings, knowing that you're rooted in a safe environment.

However, if your root chakra is out of balance, you might notice some warning signs manifesting in your emotional and physical state. One common indicator is persistent feelings of fear and anxiety. These emotions are often tied to unmet basic needs such as food, shelter, and financial security. When these fundamental aspects of survival are threatened or unfulfilled, the root chakra's energy can become blocked or distorted, leading to heightened anxiety levels and a general sense of unrest.

Increased physical ailments are another telltale sign of imbalance within the root chakra. You may experience issues such as lower back pain, leg problems, or digestive complaints, which are all areas influenced by the root chakra's energy flow. Additionally, chronic fatigue and weakened immunity could suggest that the root chakra needs attention. It's believed that, when this chakra is not functioning optimally, the body might struggle to maintain its strength and health, as it lacks the grounding force necessary for vitality.

To deepen your understanding of your root chakra's current state, self-assessment techniques can be useful. Start by reflecting on your overall sense of security and stability. Are there aspects of your life where you feel particularly anxious or fearful? Consider your physical well-being and note any recurring ailments that might link to your body's foundational systems. Journaling thoughts and emotions can help illuminate patterns related to how you feel about your safety and grounding.

Meditation can serve as a valuable tool in assessing and working towards balancing the root chakra. During meditation, you can visualize the color red, associated with this chakra, enveloping the base of your spine like a nurturing, grounding light. This practice helps bring awareness to the energy center and encourages its alignment with the rest of your chakras. Additionally, paying attention to your body's feedback during yoga or mindful movement exercises can offer clues about potential blockages or imbalances.

While scientific research on chakras remains limited, the non-tangible benefits of engaging in chakra work are embraced by many spiritual traditions. Practitioners believe that addressing the root chakra's needs can foster a greater sense of balance and connection to the Earth, contributing positively to one's mental and emotional states. For those interested in exploring this holistic approach, it's important to integrate these practices with conventional health assessments and treatments.

Grounding Exercises and Techniques to Connect with the Earth

Exploring grounding exercises and techniques can be a fulfilling journey towards stabilizing your root chakra. By connecting with nature and practicing specific physical activities, you enhance your sense of security and stability. Let's dive into some practical ways to ground yourself effectively.

Starting with nature walks, there's something uniquely rejuvenating about immersing yourself in the natural world. Whether it's a peaceful stroll through the woods or a brisk walk in a local park, the act of walking amidst nature helps release stress and promotes energetic grounding. The rhythmic pace of your footsteps combined with fresh air invigorates both body and mind, fostering a deeper connection with the Earth. This practice not only grounds you energetically but provides a mental escape from daily stressors, offering a moment of tranquility in life's hustle. To make the most of your nature walks, try being mindful of your surroundings—listen to the rustle of leaves, feel the breeze on your skin, and become aware of your feet touching the earth. This sensory engagement aids in amplifying the grounding effect.

Guided meditations focused on the root chakra offer another powerful technique for solidifying your connection to the Earth.

These meditations often involve visualization exercises that concentrate on this energy center located at the base of the spine. A common practice is to visualize a bright red light or roots extending into the earth, anchoring and grounding you. Such imagery strengthens your bond with the Earth's energies, enhancing feelings of safety and stability. If you're new to meditation, there are many resources available online or through apps where you can find guided sessions specifically targeting the root chakra. Dedicating just a few minutes daily to these meditations can cultivate a profound sense of inner peace and rootedness.

Incorporating simple yoga poses like Tadasana, or Mountain Pose, into your routine can aid in releasing stagnation while encouraging alignment. This pose, which involves standing tall with feet together and arms by your sides, creates a foundation of strength and balance. It's an excellent way to focus on posture and breath, allowing energy to flow freely throughout your body. In addition to Tadasana, other grounding poses like Warrior I and II, Tree Pose, and Garland Pose can also be beneficial. Taking time to move through these poses with intention encourages an alignment of the physical and energetic bodies, helping to stabilize the root chakra.

One of the simplest and most effective grounding techniques involves walking barefoot, a practice known as earthing. There's scientific evidence pointing to the benefits of direct contact with the ground for our health and well-being. Physically connecting with the Earth by walking barefoot on grass, soil, or sand allows you to absorb its electrons, helping to reduce inflammation, improve sleep, and elevate mood (OctoberCMS, 2024). Energetically, this practice connects you deeply with the Earth, providing a powerful form of grounding and balancing for the root chakra. Make it a habit to spend some time each week without shoes, whether in your backyard, a nearby park, or even a sandy beach, and notice how it enhances your feelings of connectedness and stability.

Additionally, exploring other physical exercises can fortify your Muladhara chakra. Activities such as jogging or dancing engage the lower parts of the body—legs and feet—which are pivotal in activating the root chakra. Regular jogging, especially in natural settings, combines repetitive physical movement with grounding energy. Dancing, whether freestyle or structured, focuses energy on leg strength and coordination, aligning physical activity with chakra activation. Similarly, gardening can be a meditative experience that grounds you as you connect directly with the Earth through touch.

As you begin to integrate these techniques into your life, remember that grounding is a personal journey. What resonates deeply with one person might not have the same impact on another, so allow yourself the freedom to explore different practices. Consistency is key; regular engagement in these grounding exercises will support sustained balance in your root chakra over time.

Nutritional Support for Root Chakra Health

When considering the health of your root chakra, nutrition is fundamental. The root chakra is deeply tied to our sense of stability and grounding, making it essential to incorporate foods that resonate with these qualities. Root vegetables like carrots, potatoes, and beets are paramount in enhancing the vitality of this energy center. These earth-toned foods not only provide grounding energy but also offer the vitamins and minerals necessary for strengthening emotional stability. Their connection to the soil imbibes them with properties believed to promote a profound sense of security and stability, crucial for a balanced root chakra.

A balanced diet isn't just about eating specific foods; it's an approach to nourish both the body and mind holistically. Incorporating a variety of food groups ensures that you receive all the nutrients needed for optimal energy levels and overall well-being. While root vegetables should play a significant role, lean proteins, whole grains, and healthy fats should also be included to keep the body's energy balanced. By focusing on diverse dietary choices, you not only support the physical body but create a foundation for emotional and spiritual stability as well. This balance allows the root chakra to function effectively, contributing to a sense of security and connection to the Earth.

Hydration might seem like a simple concept, but its importance in maintaining the balance of the root chakra cannot be overstated. Water is essential as it not only sustains bodily functions but also acts as a purifier. Keeping hydrated helps maintain energy flow through the chakras, supporting the root's ability to stabilize. Think of hydration as an anchor that keeps you grounded while allowing energy to flow freely. Drinking adequate amounts of water daily supports all bodily systems, contributing to a sense of groundedness and stability. In the context of chakras, water embodies the Earth element, reinforcing the need for proper hydration to feel connected and secure.

Mindful eating is another practice that can significantly impact the health of your root chakra. Taking a moment of gratitude before meals fosters a deeper connection between the food you consume and your body. This practice isn't just about acknowledging the food itself but also recognizing the energy and effort involved in bringing that meal to your table. Mindfulness during meals encourages a focus on the present moment, enhancing your awareness of textures, flavors, and the act of nourishing your body. This heightened consciousness strengthens the body-mind connection, promoting a sense of grounding and encouraging stability, vital for a balanced root chakra.

Incorporating mindful eating habits extends beyond gratitude. It involves being attentive to your body's hunger cues and the sensations experienced while eating. This form of conscious consumption ensures not only satisfaction from your meals but emphasizes the nurturing aspect of food. When the process of eating becomes deliberate and intentional, it creates space for reflection and appreciation, integrating emotional stability within your physical being. Thus, each meal can become a ritual of grounding, keeping the root chakra aligned with feelings of safety and steadiness.

Root Chakra Meditation (Muladhara)

Focus: Grounding, Stability, Security

Duration: 10-15 minutes

- Find a Comfortable Position: Sit or lie down in a relaxed position. Close your eyes and take a few deep breaths, allowing your body to relax with each exhale.
- Begin Visualization: Visualize a glowing red light at the base of your spine, growing stronger with each breath. Feel this red light anchoring you to the earth, like roots extending deep into the ground.
- Breathwork: Inhale deeply and imagine the red light brightening; exhale, letting go of fear and insecurity.
- Affirmation: Silently or aloud, repeat: "I am safe. I am grounded. I am secure."
- Close the Meditation: After several minutes of visualization, slowly return your awareness to your body. Gently wiggle your fingers and toes, and when you're ready, open your eyes.

The Sacral Chakra: Creativity and Emotion

Exploring the sacral chakra reveals fascinating insights into how this energy center influences our emotions and creativity. Located just below your navel, it's a hub for feelings, relationships, and self-expression. Through an informal journey, we can dive into the intriguing world of the sacral chakra, where the balance or imbalance of this energy can lead to a range of emotional experiences. Its vital role in our lives is often overlooked, yet unlocking its potential can open doors to profound understanding and personal growth. From moments of pure joy to pangs of creative block, discovering how the sacral chakra functions can illuminate paths towards enhanced well-being and enriched creativity.

As we delve deeper into the nuances of the sacral chakra, we will uncover how its balance affects not only our emotional health but also our capacity for creative expression and relationship dynamics. This chapter will guide you through recognizing the signs of imbalance, whether it's overactive with overwhelming emotions or underactive with a sense of detachment and monotony. It will examine how these extremes manifest in behaviors affecting daily life and interpersonal relations. Additionally, we'll explore practical ways to restore harmony within this chakra, leading to healthier emotional flows and inspired creativity. By the end of this exploration, you will have a clearer perspective on nurturing your sacral chakra and embracing its essential contributions to your emotional and creative landscape.

Emotional Indicators of Sacral Chakra Imbalance

Emotional balance and creativity thrive when the sacral chakra is in harmony. This energy center, often associated with sensuality, pleasure, and emotional well-being, can significantly influence our behavior and relationships. Understanding the signs of its overactivity or underactivity can enhance self-awareness and promote healing.

Overactivity in the sacral chakra often manifests as emotional excesses, such as overwhelming joy or anger. This doesn't just make one's emotions seem larger than life but also leads to impulsive actions that might disrupt daily routines or relationships. For instance, one might feel a strong urge to chase every new experience without considering the consequences, leading to chaotic behaviors. When joy knows no bounds, it can quickly turn into mania, affecting decision-making processes. Similarly, unchecked anger may cause confrontations, isolating oneself from others.

Conversely, when the sacral chakra is underactive, feelings of inadequacy and emotional detachment might surface. It's as if the vibrant hues of life fade to gray, leaving behind a sense of monotony and stagnation. This lethargic state saps motivation, making personal and professional accomplishments seem distant and unattainable. It's akin to standing knee-deep in mud — every step forward feels sluggish and burdensome. Emotional connections suffer, too, as detachment creates barriers between oneself and loved ones. Like a muted spotlight, this block dims the vibrancy of interactions, potentially causing misunderstandings and isolation.

Balancing the sacral chakra becomes essential in restoring emotional stability. When in equilibrium, this chakra allows emotions to flow freely and healthily, enhancing creative expression. Imagine a river that neither floods nor dries up; it fosters growth along its banks, supporting life and creativity. Balanced energy encourages an open mind and heart, inviting a gentle exploration of new ideas and artistic pursuits. When creativity and emotion dance hand in hand, they spark moments of inspiration and joy that are neither overwhelming nor restrained.

An imbalanced sacral chakra also plays a pivotal role in how relationship boundaries are perceived and established. A person with an overactive sacral chakra might struggle to set boundaries, displaying possessiveness or jealousy in relationships. This can lead to dramatic outbursts or dependency issues, where one seeks validation through others. On the flip side, an underactive sacral chakra might result in overly rigid boundaries, making deep connection difficult. Withdrawal into oneself can lead to misunderstanding or missed opportunities for meaningful interaction, reinforcing loneliness.

Insights into these patterns allow individuals to reassess their approach to relationships, creating healthier dynamics. Recognizing when to draw near and when to maintain space within relationships is key to forming fulfilling connections. Understanding the root causes of emotional reactions and learning to channel them constructively can be transformative. It's about finding that sweet spot where intimacy and independence coexist, where love is given and received without fear or expectation.

The journey to a balanced sacral chakra is deeply personal and requires introspection. It invites individuals to explore not only external relationships but the internal landscape of their own emotions. Simple practices like mindfulness and reflection can illuminate areas where imbalance resides, offering pathways to healing. As awareness grows, so does the capacity to transform old patterns into nurturing habits.

Incorporating activities that engage the senses can support this process. Spending time in nature, enjoying art, or indulging in gentle movement like yoga or tai chi can stimulate the sacral chakra, aligning it with one's emotional core. As individuals nurture this energy center, they cultivate not just creativity and emotional wellness, but a deeper understanding of themselves and those around them. Engaging with the sacral chakra isn't about erasing imperfections but embracing the full spectrum of human experience, fostering growth and connecting more authentically with the world.

Creative Pursuits to Stimulate Sacral Chakra Energy

When you think about fostering your creativity and seeking emotional balance, tapping into the power of the sacral chakra can be transformative. This energy center, nestled just below your navel, is pivotal for unleashing creative instincts and emotions. It's a canvas in itself—one you can nurture through various artistic endeavors.

Let's start with painting and dancing, two activities that not only promote creativity but also act as liberating forces for pent-up emotions. Imagine standing before a blank canvas or moving to the rhythm of your favorite song. Painting allows you to express colors and forms reflective of your inner world. It's an invitation to step outside of judgment and simply create. Dance, on the other hand, frees your body, allowing it to sway with abandon, releasing emotional tension while connecting with every muscle and heartbeat. The simple act of engaging in these creative expressions ignites a spark within your sacral chakra, encouraging a flow of vibrant energy that is both healing and invigorating. These artistic engagements hold the key to unlocking deeper levels of personal insight and emotional release.

Integrating natural materials in art and craft projects is another way to ground sacral energy and connect with Earth's nurturing spirit. There's something inherently soothing about working with elements of nature—like wooden beads, stones, or dried flowers—as they have an organic rhythm that resonates deeply with our own sacral vibrations. For instance, weaving a wall hanging using twigs and wool can foster a sense of grounding, as each element links you back to the earth, reminding you of the cyclical nature of life and creativity. Embracing this groundedness stabilizes your energy, amplifies your creative output, and enhances your intrinsic connection to nature's cycles.

Another profound tool for balancing the sacral chakra is maintaining a regular journaling practice. Journaling acts as a mirror reflecting your internal landscape, providing clarity and relief from emotional clutter. When you jot down thoughts, dreams, or simple reflections, you're engaging in a therapeutic process—channeling feelings into words, thereby gaining insights and perspectives that might otherwise remain hidden. Writing poetry or even penning affirmations geared towards self-love or abundance can enhance this practice further by aligning your intentions with your highest emotional aspirations.

Through storytelling, whether fictional or rooted in personal experience, you embark on visualizing scenarios that echo your emotions, crafting narratives where characters navigate challenges that resonate with your reality. This method of storytelling can empower you to articulate and explore your feelings in a safe, structured space. Writing, when used intentionally, nurtures emotional expression and offers a sanctuary for your thoughts to take form.

Collaboration is another key aspect that deserves attention. Engaging in collaborative creative endeavors, whether it's joining a writers' group or participating in community art projects, offers a unique opportunity to deepen connections with others. In these shared spaces, mutual support and inspiration fuel collective creativity, creating a rich tapestry of ideas and experiences. This melding of minds not only enhances the quality of your work but also fosters relationships that thrive on shared passion and understanding. Such interactions encourage vulnerability, trust, and a deeper appreciation of diverse perspectives—all essential ingredients for a balanced sacral chakra.

Engaging with others in creative collaborations can open new pathways for joy and fulfillment, leading to richer personal and inter-relational dynamics. The shared journey of creation breaks barriers, strengthens bonds, and cultivates a sense of belonging—a foundational need aligned with sacral energy.

Incorporating these practices into your routine can have a profound impact on your well-being, enriching your creative potential and emotional equilibrium. By embracing artistic expression, crafting with natural materials, delving into personal writing, and collaborating with like-minded souls, you tap into the essence of the sacral chakra. This lively energy center, when nurtured and balanced, serves as a catalyst for transformation, propelling you toward a life filled with passion, creativity, and joy.

Healing Through Sensory Experiences and Activities

The sacral chakra, also known as Svadhisthana, is pivotal for tapping into our creativity and emotions. It governs our ability to connect with others and derive pleasure from life. One of the most effective ways to nurture this chakra is through integrating sensory experiences into healing practices. By engaging both the physical body and emotional self, we can foster a sense of balance and well-being.

Let's dive into sensory awareness first. Sensory awareness has a profound impact on balancing the chakras, particularly the sacral chakra. It involves actively engaging with colors, sounds, and scents to evoke emotional responses that support the flow of energy. For example, surrounding yourself with the color orange, which corresponds to the sacral chakra, can help activate its energy. Whether it's incorporating orange hues into your home decor or wearing clothes in this vibrant color, these visual cues serve as gentle reminders to stimulate this energy center.

Sounds play an equally vital role. Listening to music with rhythmic beats or nature sounds like flowing water can resonate with the watery essence of the sacral chakra. These auditory stimulants not only help in soothing the mind but also promote emotional relaxation and release. Aromatherapy using essential oils such as ylang-ylang and sandalwood can further enhance this experience, offering a fragrant pathway to emotional tranquility.

Incorporating aromatherapy into daily routines can be comforting for the sacral chakra, enhancing both emotional and physical grounding. Burning incense or diffusing essential oils in a space where you spend time can create an atmosphere that promotes serenity and introspection. Aromatic baths using floral or citrus scents provide a luxurious setting for unwinding, encouraging a deeper connection with one's inner self.

Moreover, tactile activities like massaging with essential oils or engaging in creative arts that involve handcrafting can be incredibly grounding. The repetitive motion involved in kneading clay or painting allows for a meditative state, centering the mind while simultaneously stimulating the creative aspects governed by the sacral chakra.

Dance and rhythmic movements are another potent method to release emotional blockages and improve energy flow throughout the body. Various forms of dance, whether it's traditional dance or simple free-flow movement, encourage the liberation of pent-up emotions. Engaging in this form of expression allows one to physically manifest feelings, providing relief and promoting a harmonious energy flow.

Practicing mindful movement not only aids in releasing stuck emotions but also offers a way to connect with the body's natural rhythms. Techniques like Tai Chi or certain yoga poses can help align the body's energies with those of the universe, creating a symphony of movement and breath that soothes the sacral chakra's needs for flow and flexibility.

Mindful eating is another practice that celebrates flavors and nourishment, presenting food not just as sustenance but as a rich, sensory experience. By savoring each bite and appreciating the textures, aromas, and tastes of food, individuals can engage their senses fully. This form of eating not only enhances the enjoyment of meals but also fosters emotional well-being—nurturing the body's needs alongside the soul's desire for vitality and joy.

As we nourish ourselves, it's crucial to choose foods that are vibrant and full of life. Fresh fruits, especially oranges and mangoes, and spicy foods that awaken the taste buds can invigorate the sacral chakra. Including these elements in your diet contributes to a sense of satisfaction, energizing your creative and emotional centers.

Connecting back to the body through dance or mindful eating allows one to recognize the beauty in everyday actions. Each moment becomes an opportunity to express gratitude and immerse oneself in the simple pleasures of life. The sacral chakra thrives on this acknowledgement, blossoming under attention and care.

This vibrant energy center plays a crucial role in shaping how we feel and connect with others, impacting everything from emotional outbursts to feelings of detachment. Finding balance here can help us navigate through life's ups and downs more gracefully, allowing creativity and healthy relationships to flourish. By understanding what an overactive or underactive sacral chakra looks like, we gain valuable insights into our own emotional landscape and behaviors. Recognizing these patterns empowers us to create healthier dynamics in our personal and social lives, offering a path toward more fulfilling connections.

No journey is complete without tools to nourish our emotional core. Engaging in activities that stimulate the sacral chakra, like painting, dancing, or even writing, can serve as powerful outlets for pent-up emotions and creative expression. These practices, alongside sensory experiences such as aromatherapy and mindful eating, offer ways to nurture this vital energy center. Whether it's the joyful release found in dance or the grounding effect of crafting with natural materials, these actions invite a deeper understanding of ourselves and our place in the world. By embracing the full spectrum of human experience, we not only enhance our creativity and emotional well-being but also open new doors to connect with those around us.

Sacral Chakra Meditation (Svadhisthana)

Focus: Creativity, Emotions, Sexuality

Duration: 10-15 minutes

- Find a Comfortable Position: Sit with your spine straight, hands resting on your lower abdomen. Close your eyes and take a few calming breaths.
- Begin Visualization: Visualize a swirling orange light in your lower abdomen, just below your navel. This light represents the energy of creativity, pleasure, and emotional balance.
- Breathwork: Inhale deeply, allowing the orange light to expand with each breath. Exhale and release any blockages related to your emotional or creative energy.
- Affirmation: Repeat: "I embrace my creativity. I honor my emotions. I allow pleasure to flow through me."
- Close the Meditation: Gently bring your awareness back to the room. Move your body slowly, stretching your arms, and open your eyes when ready.

The Solar Plexus Chakra: Personal Power

Tapping into personal power is all about striking the right balance between confidence and decision-making, and at the heart of this process lies the solar plexus chakra. Nestled just above your navel, this energy center is a hub for self-esteem and autonomy. Imagine waking up each day with an innate sense of purpose, feeling empowered to tackle any challenges that come your way. The solar plexus chakra fuels this drive, offering you the ability to make choices not just based on fear or societal pressure, but truly from an authentic place of strength. It's fascinating how such a small part of ourselves can have such a massive impact on how we navigate our daily lives, ultimately shaping our journey through assertiveness and inner resolve.

Throughout this chapter, we'll dive deep into how the solar plexus chakra influences personal empowerment and why it plays a pivotal role in both decision-making and self-assurance. We'll explore practical ways to harness its potential, ensuring you can maximize your confidence in various life scenarios—be it setting healthy boundaries at work or finding the courage to pursue personal goals. This exploration will also touch on understanding the delicate balance between being assertive and aggressive, helping you learn how to manage interactions with others effectively while maintaining your core values. As you journey through these insights, you'll discover actionable strategies that not only enhance your command over personal power but also align your actions closely with your genuine desires. Get ready to unravel the mysteries of this chakra and unlock new levels of confidence and determination within yourself.

Impact of Personal Power on Decision-Making and Willpower

When delving into the realm of personal power and its intimate connection with assertive decision-making, the solar plexus chakra emerges as an essential player. At its core, personal power acts as a catalyst—one that fuels confidence when making choices and asserting oneself in various aspects of life. This powerful energy center, located just above your navel, governs feelings of autonomy, purpose, and control.

Imagine waking up one morning to face a potentially overwhelming schedule at work or home. The ability to tackle these challenges head-on, make necessary decisions, and execute plans without hesitation often comes from a well-balanced solar plexus energy. When this energy is strong, it empowers individuals to follow through on commitments. This tenacity bolsters productivity and focus, especially during challenging situations, leading to a cascade of accomplishments that might otherwise seem insurmountable.

Alongside productivity, individuals with a vibrant sense of personal power often possess a remarkable ability to set clear and respectful boundaries. Setting boundaries isn't just about saying "no" more often; it's about fostering relationships built on mutual respect and clear expectations. These individuals understand that healthy relationships are predicated on respecting each other's space and recognizing personal limits. This prevents codependency or avoidance scenarios where conflicts go unresolved or feelings are hurt due to unmet expectations.

A prime example of this principle can be seen in professional environments. Picture a colleague who consistently volunteers for additional tasks, eventually feeling overwhelmed and resentful. Such passive behavior might stem from a lack of confidence in asserting their limits. Over time, without setting proper boundaries, this person could face burnout. On the other hand, someone rooted in their personal power would have the confidence to communicate their capacity, ensuring sustained performance and positive interpersonal dynamics. Through assertiveness training, individuals often report significant improvements in managing workload and achieving better work-life balance (Darjan et al., 2020).

Yet, not everyone naturally exudes assertiveness, and that's okay. Building self-awareness becomes fundamental in this journey. Recognizing when confidence dwindles helps anchor decision-making in authentic desires rather than societal pressures or fears. It requires taking a step back, introspecting, and asking oneself critical questions: What do I genuinely want? Are my current actions aligned with my true values and goals? When these inquiries become part of daily life, decisions made become reflections of one's genuine self, rather than reactive responses to external stimuli.

For instance, consider someone contemplating a career change. Without self-awareness, they might succumb to doubts, second-guess their abilities, or remain stuck in an unfulfilling role out of fear of the unknown. However, by harnessing their solar plexus energy and centering their decisions around self-awareness, individuals can embark on paths aligned with their aspirations, thus transforming potential anxiety into purposeful action.

The importance of self-esteem in this context cannot be overstated. Healthy self-esteem serves as an internal compass, guiding us towards actions and choices that reinforce personal power. It's about believing in our ability to handle whatever life throws our way, embracing both successes and failures without letting them define our worth. In fact, studies have demonstrated the cyclical relationship between self-esteem and assertiveness—a boost in one often leads to an increase in the other (Darjan et al., 2020).

Harnessing one's personal power also involves understanding the intricate balance between assertiveness and aggression. Being assertive means communicating needs and desires openly and respectfully, recognizing the rights of others while standing firm on one's own. Aggressiveness, conversely, might fulfill short-term goals but often damages long-term relationships due to its domineering nature. Similarly, passive-aggression sidesteps direct communication, breeding resentment and misunderstanding over time (Mayo Clinic Staff, 2020).

Guidelines aimed at aligning actions with true desires might include reflecting on past decisions to identify patterns, seeking feedback from trusted confidants, and practicing mindfulness to stay present and aware of one's inner dialogue. By doing so, individuals can ensure that their actions resonate with their deepest values, paving the way for authentic living.

Breathing Techniques to Activate the Solar Plexus

In exploring the solar plexus chakra, or Manipura, it's essential to understand how breathing techniques can awaken and invigorate this vital energy center. The solar plexus is intimately connected with personal power, confidence, and self-esteem. Therefore, incorporating specific breathwork practices into daily routines can significantly enhance one's sense of self and vitality.

Diaphragmatic breathing serves as a foundational technique for stimulating the solar plexus chakra. It involves deep, abdominal breaths that help initiate energy flow throughout the body. This method reduces stress by activating the body's parasympathetic nervous system, which is responsible for promoting relaxation and focus. By engaging in diaphragmatic breathing, individuals can feel a renewed connection to their inner strength, enhancing their ability to concentrate on tasks and make decisions with greater confidence.

Another powerful technique is the Breath of Fire, often used in yoga and meditation practices. This rapid, rhythmic breathing exercise can accelerate energy levels and boost confidence by clearing emotional stagnation linked to low self-esteem. As you practice, you'll notice the warmth spreading throughout your abdomen, igniting feelings of empowerment and resilience. The Breath of Fire not only raises your energy but also helps release negative emotions, leaving room for positive growth and self-assurance.

Visualization plays a crucial role in harnessing the energy of the solar plexus chakra. While engaging in any breathing practice, imagine a vibrant yellow light radiating from your upper abdomen. This visualization channels the energy of the solar plexus, affirming your positive intentions and fortifying your resilience against life's challenges. Picture this light growing brighter and more intense with each breath, symbolizing the expansion of your personal power and ability to overcome obstacles.

Integrating mindful breathing exercises into daily life ensures continuous activation of the solar plexus chakra. Simple practices like taking a few moments each morning to breathe consciously or setting aside time during breaks to focus on your breath can renew your confidence and commitment to personal goals. When you make these practices a habit, you actively nurture your solar plexus energy, contributing to an overall sense of well-being and self-assuredness.

Consider beginning your day with a brief session of diaphragmatic breathing, perhaps while enjoying your morning coffee or just before starting work. Allow yourself to settle into a comfortable position, close your eyes, and take slow, deep breaths, feeling your abdomen rise and fall with each inhale and exhale. This moment of calm not only grounds you but also sets a positive tone for the day ahead.

The Breath of Fire can be particularly useful when you need an energetic boost, such as before a meeting or a challenging task. Find a quiet space, sit tall, and begin by inhaling deeply, then exhale forcefully through your nose at a brisk pace. Maintain a steady rhythm, focusing on the sensation in your abdomen, and continue for one to three minutes. This practice will leave you feeling invigorated, confident, and ready to tackle whatever lies ahead.

Lastly, do not underestimate the power of visualization. Use it as a tool to reinforce positive changes within yourself. During any breathwork session, close your eyes and picture that vibrant yellow light emanating from your solar plexus. See it as a beacon of your inner strength and determination, illuminating your path and guiding you toward your aspirations. Let this image serve as a reminder of the personal power you possess, encouraging you to embrace each day with courage and optimism.

Affirmations to Boost Self-Worth and Confidence

In the journey toward personal empowerment, affirmations serve as a powerful tool in nurturing self-esteem and reinforcing the energy of the solar plexus chakra. Each affirmation you speak has the potential to transform negative thought patterns into empowering beliefs, making it crucial for personal growth and maintaining a supportive inner dialogue.

Affirmations work by challenging and overcoming self-sabotaging thoughts, replacing them with new narratives that fuel self-confidence and personal strength. To effectively craft affirmations, one must focus on using present-tense, positive, and specific language. This approach ensures that the affirmations resonate on a personal level and continue to remain relevant over time. For instance, saying "I am capable and strong" reinforces an immediate sense of competence. Similarly, "I decide my own future" instills belief in one's ability to shape their destiny. Language shapes our reality, and using words that are clear and assertive allows us to reframe existing beliefs.

Integrating affirmations into daily routines significantly magnifies their impact. By weaving them into morning rituals or journaling practices, individuals constantly loop back to their goals and desires, fortifying self-worth and emotional well-being. Starting your day with affirmations sets a positive tone, providing a protective armor against negativity. Meanwhile, ending your day with affirmations helps embed these positive thoughts deeper into your subconscious, ensuring they are reinforced during rest.

This consistent use of affirmations is essential in boosting self-esteem, which fosters resilience and empowerment, particularly during life's challenges. In moments of doubt or hardship, having a reservoir of affirmations to draw from can make a significant difference. They become a source of unwavering support, reminding you of your innate capabilities and helping you navigate through difficult circumstances with greater ease.

In practical terms, self-esteem thrives when we feed it with affirmations that highlight our strengths and abilities. As adults interested in natural health and personal development, it's important to remember that affirmations are more than just words; they are declarations of intent and belief, paving the way for a more empowered mindset. Crafting these statements requires mindfulness and intention, ensuring they truly reflect your personal ambitions and values.

Set aside dedicated time each day to engage with your affirmations, be it during meditation or while taking a quiet moment to yourself. They should feel like a conversation with your innermost self, aligning with your goals and aspirations. Additionally, placing visual reminders around your home or workspace can help keep these affirmations at the forefront of your mind, serving as constant motivators.

The solar plexus chakra is deeply connected to our sense of individual control and autonomy. When balanced, it empowers us to make decisions with confidence and clarity. It's important to recognize that blockages in this area can stem from old fears or past experiences that undermined our sense of self. By combining affirmations with other supportive practices such as yoga, meditation, or even breathwork, you can further enhance this energy center's strength, promoting overall well-being.

Affirmations also play a vital role in setting healthy boundaries, an essential component of robust personal power. By articulating affirmations that emphasize respect and self-worth, individuals learn to assert themselves more effectively, ultimately leading to healthier interpersonal dynamics. Feeling confident in establishing boundaries stems from a strong sense of self-assurance, which regular affirmation practice can cultivate.

In essence, the regular practice of affirmations acts as a catalyst, enhancing one's ability to confront challenges and embrace opportunities with courage and assertiveness. By nurturing a compassionate inner dialogue, you create a resilient foundation that supports your personal power, ensuring you're ready to tackle whatever life throws your way with grace and confidence.

While the path to developing personal power is uniquely individual, affirmations provide a universal strategy to foster inner strength and self-belief. As you continue on this journey, remember that consistency is key. The more these affirmations are repeated and internalized, the more profound their impact will be in transforming your mindset and shaping your reality. By combining affirmations, breathwork, and visualization techniques, one can invigorate the solar plexus chakra, paving the way for personal empowerment and a more fulfilled life.

Solar Plexus Chakra Meditation (Manipura)

Focus: Confidence, Personal Power, Willpower

Duration: 10-15 minutes

- Find a Comfortable Position: Sit comfortably, spine straight. Place your hands on your upper abdomen, just below the ribcage.

- Begin Visualization: Picture a warm, bright yellow light glowing in your solar plexus area. This light represents your inner power, confidence, and strength.

- Breathwork: As you inhale, feel this yellow light expanding through your torso. With each exhale, release any self-doubt or lack of confidence.

- Affirmation: Repeat: "I am powerful. I am confident. I trust in myself."
- Close the Meditation: Slowly bring your attention back to the room, move your body gently, and open your eyes.

The Heart Chakra: Love and Connection

Exploring the heart chakra provides insight into our ability to love and connect with others. This energy center, located near the heart, governs our capacity for compassion, empathy, and balance in relationships. It serves as a pivotal element in maintaining emotional well-being and forming strong bonds with those around us. Through understanding and nurturing this chakra, individuals can enhance their personal relationships by fostering a deeper sense of love and connection. The heart chakra is often seen as the bridge between the physical and spiritual realms, allowing one to access a more profound state of consciousness. By tapping into its power, people can begin a journey toward emotional harmony and enlightenment.

In this chapter, we delve into the delicate balance of giving and receiving love within personal relationships, a key aspect influenced by the heart chakra. Readers will discover how imbalances in these dynamics can lead to challenges such as resentment or disconnect and learn ways to identify and address them effectively. The chapter will guide you through practical approaches like open communication and boundary setting, essential for fostering reciprocity and mutual respect. Additionally, we'll explore specific practices aimed at enhancing the energy of the heart chakra, such as gratitude journaling and visualization techniques. These tools help nurture emotional connections, promoting an atmosphere where love and appreciation can thrive. Through these insights and techniques, the chapter aims to equip you with the knowledge and skills to deepen your relationships, enriching both your personal life and your broader community interactions.

Balancing Giving and Receiving in Personal Relationships

Understanding the dynamics of giving and receiving love is crucial for maintaining harmony in relationships. Both giving and receiving are vital components that should be balanced, like the natural ebb and flow of tides. When one person in a relationship gives too much or receives too little, this imbalance can lead to emotional distress. Recognizing personal patterns in these dynamics can help individuals achieve a more fulfilling and equitable bond with others.

It's important to consider how our tendencies might affect the flow of energy within relationships. Some individuals naturally give more, often finding joy in caring for others. However, if their contributions aren't reciprocated, they may begin to feel underappreciated or drained. Conversely, those who receive without giving back might unwittingly cause tension or resentment in the relationship. Awareness of these patterns allows each party to adjust their approach, fostering mutual respect and understanding.

Imbalances in the dynamic often manifest through emotional blockages such as resentment, fear, or inadequacy. These feelings can cloud judgment and communication, leading to conflict and disconnect. For instance, a giver may start feeling taken for granted if their efforts go unnoticed, while receivers might feel guilty or undeserving, disrupting the flow of affection. Identifying these signs can prevent them from festering and escalating into bigger issues.

Addressing such imbalances requires practical approaches to foster reciprocity. Open and honest communication becomes essential here, where individuals express their needs and expectations without fear of judgment. This can include discussing boundaries and what each partner values most in their emotional exchanges. Mutual respect is key; it's about creating an environment where both partners feel safe to share their thoughts and feelings.

Incorporating specific practices can further enhance the energy of the heart chakra and facilitate balance in interactions. One effective method is gratitude journaling, which encourages individuals to reflect on daily moments of received kindness and their own acts of giving. This practice can shift focus onto positive experiences, subtly altering perceptions and promoting appreciation on both ends.

Visualization techniques are also recommended to nurture the heart's energy field. Imagining waves of love flowing between oneself and others can strengthen connections and open up channels for a balanced exchange of affection. Mindful breathing exercises that focus on the heart center can amplify this process, fostering a tranquil state conducive to healthy interactions.

By integrating these activities, individuals can create a thriving environment for their heart chakra, promoting emotional well-being and meaningful connections. The interchange between giving and receiving thus becomes a harmonious dance where both parties engage equally, maintaining equilibrium and enriching their relationships.

Practices for Cultivating Kindness and Empathy

To enhance kindness and empathy through the heart chakra, start by adopting mindfulness exercises. Mindfulness promotes an active and sensitive presence in our daily interactions, helping us approach each situation without judgment. By practicing techniques such as deep breathing or conscious awareness of our surroundings, we cultivate a sense of calm and focus that allows us to engage with others more empathetically. These exercises encourage us to listen actively and respond thoughtfully, fostering genuine connections.

The impact of simple acts of kindness on the heart chakra is profound, transforming both personal well-being and interpersonal relationships. Research has shown that small gestures like offering compliments, lending a helping hand, or simply smiling at someone can significantly influence our mood and health. Studies suggest that engaging in these actions increases the production of oxytocin, a hormone linked to emotional bonding and empathy. By incorporating these simple yet meaningful acts into our routine, we nurture the energy flow within the heart chakra, leading to enhanced emotional resilience and happiness.

Reflective techniques are invaluable tools for those seeking to deepen self-awareness and strengthen emotional ties within their communities. Gratitude journals, for instance, offer a practical way to shift focus from lack to abundance. By regularly noting down things we're thankful for, we become more attuned to positive experiences around us, which can improve our outlook on life and boost our ability to connect with others. Additionally, engaging in reflective meditation sessions where we visualize sending love and compassion to ourselves and others can significantly bolster heart chakra energy, promoting an environment of warmth and acceptance.

The role of self-compassion is pivotal when aiming to open the heart chakra and foster authentic empathy toward others.

When we embrace self-love, we learn to quiet our inner critic and replace harsh judgments with gentle understanding. Kristin Neff's research highlights three core elements of self-compassion: self-kindness, common humanity, and mindfulness (Fargo, 2021). Self-kindness encourages us to address our struggles with warmth rather than criticism, while recognizing our shared human experience alleviates feelings of isolation. Mindfulness allows us to view challenges objectively, preventing us from becoming overwhelmed by them.

By applying self-compassion principles, we not only enhance our emotional well-being but also create a foundation for genuine empathy. When we treat ourselves with kindness, we naturally extend this compassion to others, opening our hearts to deeper connections. Simple practices like saying affirmations such as "I am here for you" or "May I accept myself" can reinforce this mindset, enabling us to communicate more openly and build stronger relationships.

Relationships Between Heart Chakra and Forgiveness

Forgiveness is a cornerstone in the journey of maintaining balance within the heart chakra, a center that governs our ability to love and connect with others deeply. Ironically, many misconceptions surround forgiveness, often leading to unnecessary emotional blockages and imbalances in this vital energy hub. Understanding forgiveness is not synonymous with reconciliation is crucial; it doesn't imply condoning or forgetting past harms but rather involves releasing oneself from the clutches of resentment that weigh heavily on the heart chakra (Jesson, 2021). Forgiveness can instigate profound healing, allowing for unimpeded flow of energy through the chakra, which fosters love and compassion both towards oneself and others.

The process of forgiving, although seemingly straightforward, can be arduous. Several methods are available to facilitate this emotional release, each helping to alleviate the burden of hurt and anger in unique ways. Visualization techniques, where one imagines letting go of grudges and resentments, serve as powerful tools to aid in healing. Similarly, letter-writing—whether sent or unsent—offers individuals an opportunity to express their feelings in a structured manner, providing clarity and closure. These practices help dismantle emotional barriers, allowing for healthier interactions and opening pathways for renewed understanding and empathy.

An often overlooked yet equally important aspect of this process is self-forgiveness. It is common for individuals who have experienced trauma or failure to place undue blame on themselves, holding onto guilt and self-recrimination long after events have passed. However, forgiving oneself is essential for achieving emotional freedom and maintaining a balanced heart chakra. This step can be incredibly challenging, requiring individuals to confront inner dialogues and perceptions that may perpetuate pain. By acknowledging personal mistakes and choosing to forgive oneself, a person can liberate their heart, fostering a sense of peace and acceptance necessary for holistic emotional health.

Practicing forgiveness holds transformative potential beyond individual healing, extending its impact to relationships and broader social dynamics. It is not merely a personal journey but an empowering act that can revive fractured ties and foster positive change in communal interactions. Embracing forgiveness cultivates an environment where love and understanding prevail over bitterness and conflict, creating space for stronger bonds and mutual growth. Over time, these acts contribute to a more compassionate society, where individuals are encouraged to embrace empathy and harmony, enriching the collective spirit.

To truly appreciate the role of forgiveness in balancing the heart chakra, consider its effects both personally and socially. On a micro level, releasing negative emotions associated with grievances allows for a more vibrant and open-hearted existence. People find themselves better equipped to engage meaningfully with others, free from past burdens that once hindered their capacity to connect. On a grander scale, embracing forgiveness promotes communal well-being, inviting individuals into a shared experience of healing and transformation. This dynamic serves as a catalyst for societal evolution, shaping a world where compassion, respect, and love are paramount values nurtured by all.

While forgiveness does not demand that wrongdoings be forgotten or relationships restored to their original state, it offers a pathway to inner liberation and external growth. By acknowledging and actively addressing pain, individuals create opportunities to evolve emotionally and spiritually, enhancing the balance and vitality of the heart chakra. As people undertake this journey, they eventually unlock deeper levels of connection and joy, reshaping personal and collective realities in profound and meaningful ways.

From gratitude journaling and visualization techniques to practicing mindfulness and self-compassion, these activities encourage a vibrant heart energy flow. Forgiveness, both towards oneself and others, plays a pivotal role in releasing emotional blockages, enabling individuals to experience deeper connections and personal growth. By integrating these practices into daily life, we create an environment where empathy, love, and meaningful connections thrive.

Heart Chakra Meditation (Anahata)

Focus: Love, Compassion, Forgiveness

Duration: 10-15 minutes

- Find a Comfortable Position: Sit or lie down, placing your hands over your heart center.
- Begin Visualization: Visualize a vibrant green light glowing in your chest. This light is the energy of unconditional love, compassion, and healing.
- Breathwork: Inhale deeply, allowing the green light to grow brighter and expand outward. Exhale, letting go of any emotional pain or resentment.

- Affirmation: Repeat: "I am love. I am compassionate. I forgive myself and others."

- Close the Meditation: Slowly become aware of your physical body, move your hands and feet, and open your eyes when you feel ready.

The Throat Chakra: Expression and Communication

Expressing oneself clearly can be an art, and this chapter delves into the vibrant world of the throat chakra, pivotal in ensuring our voices not only reach others but resonate with sincerity. Imagine unlocking a wellspring of thoughts, ideas, and emotions that have the power to shape relationships and elevate your emotional health. This journey is not merely about finding one's voice; it's about nurturing a robust vocal presence that transforms communication into a powerful tool for connection and understanding. The throat chakra sits at the heart of this exploration, urging us to express what truly matters.

We'll explore how sharpening vocal expression results in genuine truthfulness that commands attention. You will find practical advice on daily exercises that enhance vocal clarity and resonance, akin to tuning a musical instrument to hit all the right notes naturally. We'll also venture into mental practices harnessing affirmations to empower you from within, setting a positive mindset that encourages open and confident communication. Moreover, our discussion will uncover the reflective exercises that contribute to understanding yourself, enabling authentic exchanges with others. Additionally, we'll touch upon mindful speaking as a way to respect both our words and emotions, fostering dialogues filled with meaning and respect. Through these insights and techniques, you're invited to embrace your authentic voice, enriching your interactions and personal growth.

Techniques to Improve Vocal Expression and Authenticity

Unlocking the potential of the throat chakra involves not only finding your voice but enhancing its power and authenticity. A robust vocal presence not only ensures effective communication but also leaves lasting impressions on others and can significantly impact personal and professional interactions. Let's delve into practical ways to cultivate this vocal strength and express genuine truthfulness in communication.

To begin, incorporating regular voice exercises into your routine can make a substantial difference. Much like athletes who train to improve their performance, nurturing your vocal abilities through targeted exercises is essential for clarity and resonance. Simple practices such as humming, lip trills, and vowel sounds are foundational exercises that can be seamlessly integrated into daily life. These exercises work by relaxing the vocal cords, improving breath control, and enhancing articulation. Over time, they build a stronger, more controlled voice that naturally projects confidence, impacting how others perceive you. Rather than seeking complex solutions, start gently. Dedicate a few minutes each day to these exercises, gradually increasing duration as your comfort level grows.

However, refining your voice is not solely about physical exercises. The mental aspect of communication plays an equally vital role. Affirmation practices can transform negative mindsets that often hinder open expression. By regularly repeating positive affirmations, you can reinforce self-worth and truthfulness, allowing you to speak from a place of empowerment. Consider starting your day with affirmations such as, "My voice matters," or "I communicate clearly and confidently." This practice helps in silencing the internal critic, shifting focus to what truly matters—honest and impactful communication.

Moreover, true authenticity in communication begins with self-reflection. Journaling offers a path to explore and clarify personal truths. Writing down thoughts allows individuals to organize complex emotions and ideas, leading to clearer verbal expression. This reflective practice aids in understanding oneself better and communicating those insights effectively to others, fostering honesty in your dialogues. You might dedicate a few quiet moments each evening to write freely about your day, emotions, or upcoming conversations that require thoughtful preparation.

Another key strategy is mindful speaking techniques. These promote respectful dialogue and ensure your words respect both your own emotions and those of your conversation partner. Mindful speaking involves active listening, pausing before responding, and choosing words thoughtfully. It's about being present in the conversation and fully aware of the emotional undercurrents at play. Try practicing this by slowing down during discussions, giving yourself time to absorb what's been said and respond mindfully.

Listening Skills as Part of Healthy Throat Chakra Activity

Listening is not just about hearing words; it's an essential practice that influences our communication and balances the throat chakra. In today's fast-paced world, effective communication is often overshadowed by distractions and misunderstandings. However, listening plays a crucial role in maintaining not only harmony in our interactions but also the equilibrium of the throat chakra, which governs expression and truth-telling.

Active listening is where our journey begins. It involves more than simply catching the words spoken by others. By truly concentrating on what the other person is saying, we open ourselves up to understanding their emotions and perspectives. Techniques such as nodding, asking clarifying questions, and summarizing what you've heard can foster empathy and strengthen relationships. Through this engaged form of listening, we encourage open dialogue and demonstrate respect for the speaker, making them feel valued and understood. For example, when a friend shares their worries, practicing active listening can help you respond with empathy, thus enhancing your bond.

Reflective listening takes the act a step further. This technique focuses on paraphrasing and reflecting back what someone has said, a strategy that validates their feelings and shows genuine interest. Reflective listening aids in diffusing conflicts by ensuring everyone feels heard, thereby building trust. It helps manage misunderstandings and encourages openness. In situations where emotions run high, such as in family disputes or workplace discussions, reflecting what others say can create an environment where people feel safe to share their thoughts without fear of judgment.

Equally important is recognizing non-verbal cues. These include body language, facial expressions, and even silence. Non-verbal signals often reveal true feelings that words might mask, providing deeper insights into the speaker's emotional state. For instance, crossed arms might indicate defensiveness even if the words are polite. Understanding these cues enables us to respond appropriately. Being aware of such signals enhances communication by aligning our responses with the unspoken parts of conversation, bridging gaps between verbal and non-verbal communication.

Creating safe spaces is another vital aspect of fostering meaningful interactions and maintaining a balanced throat chakra. Safe spaces allow individuals to express themselves freely without the fear of criticism or backlash. Whether it's at home, work, or social gatherings, establishing environments that encourage open and honest communication nurtures growth and deeper connections. Guidelines such as setting ground rules for discussions, encouraging all voices to be heard, and agreeing on respectful disagreement can transform any space into one where expression is welcomed. When people feel they have a safe space, they are more likely to share ideas and concerns openly.

Impact of Honest Communication on Personal Growth

Honest communication and the practice of authenticity are crucial for individual development and transformation. At the heart of this process is emotional honesty, which allows individuals to explore their true selves without fear or pretense. By being honest with oneself and others, we embark on a journey of self-discovery that reveals our genuine feelings and motivations.

Emotional honesty acts as a gateway to healing, providing an avenue through which emotions can be processed and released. This openness not only aids in personal healing but also lays the groundwork for building meaningful relationships. When individuals express their true emotions, they create a space where trust and intimacy can flourish. For example, consider a person who openly discusses their anxieties about a new job. Such candor invites understanding and support from friends or partners, strengthening those connections.

Feedback is another transformative element in promoting personal growth. Constructive feedback fosters resilience, encouraging an awareness of one's communication styles and areas needing improvement. It plays a pivotal role in personal development by offering insights that might otherwise remain hidden. Engaging with feedback helps individuals understand not just how they communicate but also how their message is received by others. This interaction cultivates a deeper understanding among peers, as individuals learn to appreciate diverse perspectives and refine their own communicative approaches over time.

Setting healthy boundaries is essential for maintaining trust and personal space, serving as a foundation for well-balanced relationships. Clear boundaries protect individuals from feeling overwhelmed or intruded upon, creating an environment where open engagement is possible without the fear of overstepping limits. In both personal and professional contexts, boundaries ensure that interactions remain respectful and mutually beneficial. They help maintain balance, allowing each party to feel valued and understood, while safeguarding personal well-being.

A practical guideline for setting boundaries involves understanding one's limits and clearly communicating these to others. For instance, if workload becomes excessive at work, learning to say no or delegating tasks can preserve one's energy and prevent burnout. This proactive approach not only protects individual well-being but also enhances trust within the team, as colleagues know exactly what to expect and respect established boundaries.

Transformative storytelling is a powerful tool for promoting clarity and authenticity in communication. Sharing personal narratives can serve as a catalyst for reflection and insight into one's growth journey. When individuals recount their experiences, they not only connect with others on a deeper level but also gain a better understanding of their own paths. This storytelling becomes an instrument for empowerment, inspiring others to reflect on their journeys and consider the lessons embedded within them.

Through personal stories, individuals reveal vulnerabilities and strengths alike, fostering a sense of community and shared experience. Consider someone narrating their challenges with public speaking and how they overcame them. This narrative not only inspires listeners but encourages introspection, prompting them to examine similar hurdles in their lives.

Incorporating these elements into daily life requires practice and patience. Emotional honesty demands the courage to confront uncomfortable truths and share them with transparency. Feedback should be approached with an open mind, viewing criticism not as a setback but as an opportunity for growth. Setting boundaries calls for assertiveness and clarity, ensuring that personal limits are respected and maintained. Meanwhile, storytelling requires vulnerability, inviting others into one's inner world while laying bare the lessons learned along the way.

Techniques like active and reflective listening, combined with an awareness of non-verbal cues, enable deeper connections and trust. Creating safe spaces for open dialogue further encourages honest communication, which is essential for personal growth. As we continue on this journey of self-discovery, embracing these practices will empower us to express ourselves more authentically and engage others with empathy and understanding.

Throat Chakra Meditation (Vishuddha)
Focus: Communication, Self-Expression, Truth

Duration: 10-15 minutes

- Find a Comfortable Position: Sit comfortably with your hands resting gently at your throat.

- Begin Visualization: Visualize a clear blue light at the center of your throat, radiating outward. This light represents your ability to communicate and express your truth.

- Breathwork: With each inhale, imagine the blue light expanding and clearing any blockages. As you exhale, release any fears related to self-expression or communication.

- Affirmation: Repeat: "I speak my truth. I express myself clearly and confidently."
- Close the Meditation: Slowly bring your awareness back to your surroundings. Gently move your body, stretch, and open your eyes.

The Third Eye Chakra: Intuition and Insight

Tapping into the power of your third eye chakra is an exciting journey toward enhancing intuition and gaining deeper insights into yourself. This chakra, nestled between your eyebrows, is like a gateway to inner wisdom and clarity. But how do you unlock its full potential? You might feel drawn to explore these hidden aspects of your mind, eager to discover the intuitive gifts waiting within. It's about finding that delicate balance where your mind opens up to guidance, allowing those quiet nudges and inner voices to come alive with purpose.

In this chapter, we'll delve into practical meditation practices designed to enhance your intuitive capabilities. From mindfulness meditation to guided visualizations, these techniques aim to clear mental clutter and bring forth clarity.

You'll learn about chakra-focused meditations specifically targeted at stimulating your third eye. Plus, we'll discuss the importance of silencing daily noise so you can listen more closely to your inner self. Each method offers unique insights and can lead to profound transformations in how you perceive the world and your place in it. Whether you're a seasoned meditator or new to the practice, these approaches will pave the way for richer connections with your intuitive mind and help you navigate life's complexities with newfound confidence and understanding.

Meditation Practices to Enhance Intuitive Capabilities

Connecting with your third eye chakra can unlock your intuition and insight, bringing clarity into your life. Through targeted meditation practices, you can access deeper layers of wisdom within yourself. Let's explore different methods to enhance these intuitive abilities.

First, let's talk about mindfulness meditation, a simple yet powerful tool. This practice is all about being present in the moment. Picture yourself sitting comfortably, focusing solely on your breath as it flows in and out. Allow thoughts to come and go without clinging to them. By honing this skill, you become more sensitive to subtle inner guidance. Mindfulness sharpens your awareness, allowing you to notice those quiet nudges that usually go unnoticed. Over time, this cultivates greater clarity and understanding of your intuitive voice.

Moving on, guided visualizations offer another enriching path. Imagine a serene space where you feel comfortable and safe. Visualize your third eye chakra, located between your eyebrows, beginning to open like a radiant lotus. As you breathe deeply, envision a stream of indigo light illuminating your mind, bringing forth intuitive wisdom. This imagery helps in accessing insights that are otherwise hidden from your everyday consciousness. Embrace this practice regularly to create a direct link with your intuitive self, shedding light on decisions and paths forward.

Next, we have chakra-focused meditation. Here, the goal is to specifically stimulate your third eye chakra's energy. Begin by finding a calm spot for meditation, drawing your attention inward. Focus on your third eye area, perhaps imagining a gentle spiral of energy radiating from it. As you meditate, notice any sensations or images that arise without judgment, just observing them. This focus can awaken dormant intuitive abilities, making access to higher knowledge much more accessible.

Quieting the mind is equally crucial. In our often hectic lives, the mind is like a cluttered room, filled with distracting thoughts. Learning to silence this chatter creates space for deeper connections. Start by setting aside moments each day to simply be still. Use breathing techniques to center yourself, letting go of tension and mental noise. As thoughts clamor for attention, let them drift away like clouds in the sky, returning always to the peaceful rhythm of your breath. The quietude that follows allows your intuition to speak more clearly, revealing truths that guide your life's journey.

These meditation practices can transform how you connect with your inner self. Each method offers unique benefits that collectively enhance your intuitive perception. It's important to approach these practices with patience and openness. Consistency is key; even short daily sessions can lead to profound insights over time. Remember, intuition thrives in an environment of trust and patience. By nurturing your third eye chakra, you're not only developing stronger intuitive skills but also deepening your relationship with your true self.

Meditation isn't just about achieving tranquility; it's about tapping into the vast reservoir of potential within you. Each session brings new discoveries, uncovering hidden capabilities and helping you navigate life's complexities with a clearer perspective. Whether you're seeking answers to specific questions or simply wish to understand your innermost desires, these practices pave the way to profound self-discovery and empowerment.

To further enrich your journey, consider integrating other supportive activities, such as journaling. Reflect on your meditation experiences, noting any intuitive hits or patterns that emerge. This practice enhances your understanding and appreciation of the wisdom you gain. Also, engage with community or workshops focused on intuition and meditation, expanding your knowledge and connecting with others on similar paths. Sharing experiences and learning from one another can deepen your practice.

Decoding Dreams and Symbols in Third Eye Development

Understanding dreams and symbols is like opening a window to our subconscious, revealing hidden messages and offering profound personal insights. Through the third eye chakra, we tap into this vast realm of intuition and insight, unlocking deeper aspects of oneself. This journey begins with keeping a dream journal, which serves as a tool to capture those fleeting images and themes that dance through our minds at night.

A dream journal acts as a bridge between our conscious and subconscious worlds, enabling us to piece together the chaos of dreams into coherent narratives. Upon waking, it's essential to record dreams immediately, before they slip away. Begin by jotting down everything you recall: the vivid symbols, fleeting emotions, and even the colors that stood out. Over time, patterns begin to emerge. It might be recurring symbols or familiar themes that pop up night after night. These elements often carry significant meaning, acting as compasses pointing towards areas in your life needing attention or healing (*Dream Therapy, Dream Dictionary | Peacefulmind.com* , 2020).

Once you have maintained a dream journal for several months, take time to analyze these recordings. Identify recurring symbols and themes; maybe it's water appearing in various forms, or frequent flying experiences that need closer examination. Each symbol holds potential keys to understanding your inner world. The act of interpreting these symbols requires diving deeper than surface-level meanings. For instance, water could symbolize emotions or change, depending on its context in your dream. By looking beyond obvious interpretations, you can gain insights into unresolved feelings or desires, thus enhancing self-awareness.

Symbols are not mere images; they are layered with meanings shaped by our personal experiences and cultural backgrounds. Therefore, interpreting them might initially seem daunting. However, employing techniques such as free association—where one writes down words spontaneously associated with each symbol—can illuminate their significance. This practice invites introspection and encourages a dialogue between your conscious mind and the subconscious realm, often leading to aha moments about your life situations and emotional states.

Lucid dreaming presents another fascinating avenue for exploring and enhancing intuition. In lucid dreams, you become aware that you are dreaming and can consciously influence the narrative. Imagine realizing mid-dream that you hold the reins, deciding where to go and what to explore. This offers a unique opportunity to face fears, rehearse real-life situations, or simply revel in the creative playground of your mind. To enter a lucid dream state, start by practicing reality checks during the day.

Look at your hands or ask yourself if you're dreaming, reinforcing this habit so it eventually carries over into your dreams.

Moreover, setting intentions before sleep can increase the likelihood of having a lucid dream. Tell yourself clearly what you want to experience in your dreams. With time and practice, navigating lucid dreams becomes less about escapism and more about exploring the depths of your intuition, boosting confidence in your ability to harness the power of your subconscious mind.

Next, delving into archetypes provides yet another layer of understanding dream symbols. Coined by Carl Jung, archetypes are universal symbols present across cultures and history, rooted in what he termed the "collective unconscious." These symbols—like the hero, the mother, or the trickster—embody fundamental human experiences and traits. Exploring archetypes allows access to a shared human library of symbols, enriching your personal dream work with global insights (*Dream Interpretations, Dream Symbols, Meanings | Peacefulmind.com* , 2020).

Connecting with archetypes involves identifying which characters or scenarios repeatedly appear in your dreams. Are there figures resembling wise sages guiding you, or shadowy characters challenging your path? Once recognized, reflect on how these archetypal figures relate to your life's journey. They might represent aspects of yourself that need embracing or confronting, helping to integrate different dimensions of your personality into a harmonious whole.

Furthermore, engaging with archetypes through storytelling or journaling can deepen these connections. Write short stories inspired by these dream characters or draw illustrations capturing their essence. This creative exploration not only enhances personal insights but also fosters a greater sense of belonging within the tapestry of human experiences.

Dreams hold an intrinsic connection to our third eye chakra, the energetic center associated with intuition and inner wisdom. Activating this chakra can enhance your ability to remember and interpret dreams. Simple practices such as meditation or visualization exercises focusing on this area can open new channels of insight. Picture a radiant indigo light at the center of your forehead, growing brighter with each deep breath, inviting clarity and intuitive guidance into your consciousness.

Releasing Negative Thoughts to Clear Mental Clutter

When exploring the third eye chakra, one finds themselves on a journey toward unlocking intuition and connecting deeper with their inner wisdom. A crucial step in this journey involves recognizing and releasing limiting beliefs and negative thoughts that act as barriers to our intuitive capabilities. It might sound intimidating at first, but by focusing on specific strategies, we can dismantle these blocks effectively.

First, identifying negative thought patterns is key. These patterns often operate quietly in the background, influencing how we feel and behave without our conscious awareness. For example, you might repeatedly tell yourself, "I'm not good enough," or question your decisions with a persistent "What if I fail?" Such thoughts create mental clutter, obstructing clear intuitive signals. By bringing these negative patterns into focus, we gain the power to address them head-on. Start by jotting down your recurring thoughts for a week. Notice which ones erode your confidence or halt your inner guidance system. Once highlighted, these patterns lose some of their control over you, paving the way for transformative change.

The next step involves cognitive reframing. This technique requires challenging negative beliefs and transforming them into more empowering perspectives. Suppose you cling to the belief that you are undeserving of success. In that case, cognitive reframing encourages you to shift from "I am not good enough" to "I am capable and deserving of all life's opportunities." By asking critical questions about the validity of your negative beliefs —such as "Is there real evidence supporting this belief?" or "What would I say to a friend who felt this way?"—you begin to see these thoughts in a new light. During my own experience, reframing my limiting belief that I couldn't speak publicly without fear was liberating. By visualizing myself confidently addressing a group, I slowly replaced anxiety with anticipation and empowerment.

Affirmations for intuition serve as a vital tool to continue nurturing self-trust and positivity. Think of affirmations as planting seeds of encouraging statements in the fertile soil of your subconscious. Replace any negative self-talk with affirmations like "I trust my inner wisdom" or "My intuition guides me to my highest good." It's best to create affirmations that resonate personally and repeat them daily, preferably during moments of calm or meditation. Through consistency, these affirmations can transform your internal dialogue, encouraging a natural flow of intuitive insights.

Visualization for release is a powerful technique where imagery plays a central role in letting go of negativity. Visualization allows you to imagine scenarios that help cleanse the mind and create space for positive energy. Picture yourself standing near a flowing river; as you release each negative thought, it drifts away on the water's surface. Alternatively, visualize a radiant light enveloping you, dissolving any lingering doubts. The process of letting go visually can be incredibly cathartic, offering relief from mental burdens and enhancing your capacity for receiving intuitive messages. Sarah, a close friend, used visualization to overcome creative blocks. She imagined herself shedding heavy chains of doubt and stepping into an open field filled with endless possibilities. Her creativity flourished soon after.

To reinforce these practices, it's beneficial to include guidelines for application. For identifying negative thought patterns, maintain a journal and set aside time each evening to reflect on your day's thoughts. With cognitive reframing, try revisiting your list of negative thoughts weekly, actively working through two or three with alternative perspectives. As for affirmations, commit to three repetitions every morning and night, using a gentle, empowering tone. When practicing visualization, create a serene environment free from interruptions and allow yourself ten minutes daily to engage fully in the imagery process.

Recognizing and releasing limiting beliefs is an ongoing practice essential to deepening your connection with the third eye chakra. Each technique, when applied consistently, helps clear the path for enhanced intuition and personal insight. Rather than being obstructed by the chaos of external noise and internal uncertainty, find solace in knowing that with focus and intention, your intuitive abilities can shine through, guiding you towards growth and enlightenment.

Bringing It All Together

Opening your third eye chakra is a transformative journey into understanding your own intuitive abilities. Mindfulness meditation serves as a foundational tool, helping you remain present and sensitive to subtle internal cues. Guided visualizations provide vivid pathways to access deep-seated insights, while chakra-focused meditation invites you to awaken dormant intuitive powers. By quieting the mental noise, you allow space for intuitive messages to surface, enriching your decision-making process and life path. Each practice offers unique benefits, contributing collectively to clearer perception and deeper self-discovery.

As you integrate these methods into daily life, remember that consistency and patience are key. Meditation becomes a doorway to untapped potential, revealing hidden capabilities with each session. It's not just about finding peace but also about embracing your truest self and navigating life's challenges with newfound clarity. Whether it's through regular journaling of your experiences or engaging with like-minded communities, these supportive activities can enhance your journey. Embrace this connection with your third eye chakra as it strengthens your relationship with intuition, guiding you toward empowerment and fulfillment in ways you may never have imagined.

Third Eye Chakra Meditation (Ajna)

Focus: Intuition, Inner Wisdom, Clarity

Duration: 10-15 minutes

- Find a Comfortable Position: Sit with your spine straight and eyes closed. Focus on the space between your eyebrows.
- Begin Visualization: Picture a deep indigo light forming at your third eye, the space between your brows. This light represents your inner wisdom and intuition.

- Breathwork: As you inhale, feel the indigo light growing brighter, clearing your mind and enhancing your intuition. Exhale any confusion or mental clutter.

- Affirmation: Repeat: "I trust my intuition. I see clearly. I am connected to my inner wisdom."

- Close the Meditation: Gradually bring your awareness back to the present moment. Open your eyes when you feel ready.

The Crown Chakra: Spirituality and Enlightenment

The crown chakra is the gateway to a world beyond our everyday existence. It's where spirituality meets enlightenment, offering us a chance to connect with something greater than ourselves. This connection isn't just an abstract idea; it's an experience that can transform our lives if we open ourselves to it. By focusing on this chakra, we tap into a realm of pure consciousness and unity with the universe. For those curious about what reaching spiritual heights feels like, exploring the crown chakra is a journey worth taking.

In this chapter, we'll delve into the roles of prayer and meditation as pathways to accessing the power of the crown chakra. We'll uncover how these practices do more than just calm the mind—they act as bridges to higher realms of awareness. Learn how visualization techniques can deepen your experience, allowing you to feel connected to every part of the cosmic puzzle. Creating a sacred space for these practices will be another focus, showing how environment and setting intention can enhance and maintain your spiritual growth. Through practical advice and thoughtful exploration, this chapter offers insights into using these tools to elevate your consciousness, helping guide you toward a profound sense of peace and interconnectedness.

Connecting with Universal Consciousness through Prayer and Meditation

In the labyrinth of spirituality, prayer and meditation are often seen as guiding beacons leading individuals towards a deeper connection with universal consciousness. The crown chakra plays an integral role in this journey, acting as the spiritual gateway for awakening and connecting to higher realms. These practices elevate our awareness and foster a sense of unity with the divine.

Prayer can be seen as a heartfelt conversation between individuals and the divine. It serves as a tool to elevate one's consciousness by opening channels to a higher power or universal energy. When individuals engage in prayer, they set spiritual intentions that act like a compass pointing towards enlightenment and transcendence. Whether whispered in solitude or shared in communal worship, prayer's primary function remains to connect the soul with something far greater than itself, allowing individuals to express gratitude, seek guidance, or simply find solace.

Meditation techniques specifically targeting the crown chakra are instrumental in enhancing mindfulness and spiritual awareness. The crown chakra, located at the top of the head, is associated with pure consciousness and oneness with the universe. By focusing on this chakra during meditation, practitioners can experience heightened states of awareness and a profound sense of peace. Techniques such as mindful breathing and visualization can help channel energies through this chakra, facilitating a deeper connection with the cosmos. In essence, these techniques open the doors to universal consciousness, where one can tap into wisdom beyond ordinary perception.

Visualization acts as a powerful tool within meditation to deepen experiences of unity and spiritual awakening. Guided imagery, where practitioners visualize light or energy flowing into the crown chakra, can evoke profound sensations of connectivity with the universe. This practice not only enhances personal spiritual journeys but also cultivates a sense of interconnectedness with all living beings. Visualization guides the mind away from mundane distractions and into a realm where the lines between the self and the universe blur, offering glimpses of pure enlightenment.

Creating a sacred space for these practices is crucial for fostering consistency and deepening spiritual connections. A sacred space doesn't necessarily require an elaborate setup; it can be any quiet corner filled with items that bring peace and focus, like candles, crystals, or calming scents. Having such a dedicated area encourages regular practice, essential for maintaining a steady path toward spiritual growth. When one consistently enters this sacred environment, it signals the mind and spirit to transition into a state of mindfulness and openness, ready to receive the divine.

Guidelines for creating an effective sacred space include selecting a location that feels tranquil and free from disruptions. Personalizing this space with symbols or objects that resonate spiritually can transform it into a sanctuary of peace. Additionally, setting aside specific times for prayer and meditation can make these practices habitual, weaving them seamlessly into daily life. This consistent engagement amplifies their benefits, reinforcing one's commitment to spiritual exploration.

The journey towards universal consciousness is deeply evolving, where prayer and meditation serve as essential tools in bridging the gap between the earthly and the divine. Through prayer, individuals elevate their consciousness, reaching out to the universe with intentionality and faith. Meditation, particularly when focused on the crown chakra, sharpens this connection by cultivating mindfulness and spiritual awareness. Visualization further enriches the process, drawing practitioners closer to experiences of unity and awakening.

Balancing Ego with Higher Consciousness

Balancing the ego and higher consciousness is fundamental to achieving meaningful spiritual growth. In exploring this, we first need to recognize the dual role of the ego in our lives. Often misunderstood merely as an obstacle to enlightenment, the ego also serves essential functions that protect us. It's important to appreciate how the ego aims to keep us safe by maintaining a sense of identity and boundaries. This aspect of the ego can often create a sense of separation from others or from universal truths, yet it's not inherently negative. For example, when you encounter a situation that feels threatening, whether emotionally or physically, your ego steps in with doubts or fears, attempting to shield you from potential harm.

Understanding this protective mechanism enables us to work with the ego rather than against it. By acknowledging its presence and purpose, we prevent the ego from dominating our thoughts and actions. Instead, we allow it to exist as a managed companion as we journey towards higher consciousness. This recognition is the first step toward achieving balance—accepting both the light and shadows within us as necessary parts of our human experience.

To harmonize the ego and higher consciousness, incorporating specific techniques can be profoundly beneficial. Journaling provides a space to reflect on our experiences and emotions, allowing us to identify patterns driven by the ego's fears and insecurities. Through writing, we can clarify our thoughts and examine them from a place of consciousness rather than reaction. Another effective practice is performing acts of service. Engaging in selfless activities fosters humility by shifting the focus from ourselves to the needs of others. This redirection helps diminish the ego's grip, as we learn to appreciate the interconnectedness of all beings.

Unity consciousness, which emerges from the balance of ego and higher consciousness, encourages a deep sense of empathy and compassion. When we tap into this state, we begin to see beyond individual desires and ego-driven narratives. We start to perceive ourselves as integral parts of a larger whole, fostering relationships that are nurturing rather than competitive. Unity consciousness invites us to approach life from a perspective of shared humanity, enhancing our capacity for love and understanding. As we integrate this awareness into our daily interactions, we contribute to a more compassionate world, one small action at a time.

Another vital component in balancing the ego with higher consciousness is the practice of surrendering control and trusting the universe. Surrender does not mean giving up but rather releasing the need to dominate every aspect of life. It's about recognizing that there are forces beyond our understanding that guide us toward spiritual maturity. Surrender involves accepting uncertainty and finding peace in the unknown. By trusting that everything unfolds in divine timing, we learn patience and fortitude—a hallmark of spiritual growth.

Surrender also involves listening to inner guidance, often referred to as intuition or the voice of the soul. Cultivating this trust requires letting go of the ego's insistent demands for immediate answers or gratification. The ego thrives on certainty and predictability, making it challenging to embrace the unpredictability inherent in spiritual journeys. Yet, as we practice letting go, we develop resilience and adaptability, opening ourselves to experiences that enrich our spiritual paths.

The journey of balancing the ego and higher consciousness doesn't happen overnight; it's a gradual process requiring consistent effort and mindfulness. As we become adept at managing the ego's influence, we find more room to engage with the higher aspects of consciousness. This transformation manifests as heightened awareness—an ability to observe thoughts without judgment and to respond to life's challenges with grace rather than react impulsively. Such awareness allows us to live authentically, aligning our actions with our true selves rather than succumbing to egoic pressures.

Integration is the ultimate goal of balancing these forces—where ego and consciousness coexist in harmony. Rather than viewing the ego as an adversary, we acknowledge it as part of the whole, deserving of kindness and understanding. This compassionate approach promotes inner peace and liberation, freeing us from the internal tug-of-war between fear and love, separation and unity.

Through this harmonious balance, we embark on a path of continual growth and discovery. Each moment becomes an opportunity to deepen our relationship with ourselves and the universe. The crown chakra, symbolic of our connection to spirituality and enlightenment, flourishes when supported by a well-balanced ego and conscious awareness.

Integrating Chakra Work into Daily Life for Sustained Spiritual Growth

Nurturing sustained spiritual growth through practical chakra work is a journey that anyone can embark on with daily rituals, connections to nature, understanding of crystals and essential oils, and community involvement. Each element plays a vital role in aligning our crown chakra and enhancing our spiritual insights and universal connection.

Beginning with the foundation of daily rituals, incorporating meditation and mindfulness practices can be profoundly transformative. These rituals do not have to be intricate or time-consuming; simple acts like morning meditations or mindful breathing exercises can suffice. Every morning, setting aside ten minutes for meditation creates a sacred space within ourselves that invites peace and clarity. This is an opportunity to tune into the energy at the crown of your head, and align yourself with higher consciousness. Through consistent practice, you develop a stronger connection with your spiritual insights, gaining clarity and intuition that guide your daily life.

Mindfulness practice extends beyond formal meditation sessions and weaves into every moment of your day. Living mindfully means being fully present in each activity, whether it's savoring your breakfast, walking through a park, or even working on a task. Practicing mindfulness enriches our experience, allowing us to notice the subtle details and maintain a sense of calm, which supports spiritual growth by keeping us connected to our inner selves and the universe around us.

Connecting with nature serves as another powerful tool in strengthening our relationship with the universe. Nature acts as both a mirror and a guide to our spiritual existence. The simple act of spending time outdoors, touching the earth, listening to birdsong, or watching the clouds drift can instill a sense of wonder and awareness. Practices such as earthing—walking barefoot on grass—allow us to directly connect and receive Earth's grounding energy. This connection not only calms the mind but also harmonizes our physical and spiritual energies. Nature has a unique way of reminding us of the interconnectedness of all living things, urging us to look beyond our personal narrative and realize our place in the larger tapestry of life.

Crystals and essential oils are additional allies in our quest to balance and energize the crown chakra. Amethyst, renowned for its spiritual properties, helps in cleansing the aura and providing clarity of mind. Placing it under your pillow or holding it during meditation can enhance these effects. Similarly, essential oils like frankincense promote mental peace and spiritual awareness. By diffusing these oils during meditation or applying them diluted on pulse points, we can invite more receptive states and open our crown chakra further.

Community support also plays a significant role in nurturing spiritual growth. As social beings, sharing experiences and insights can deepen our understanding and growth. Joining group meditations or participating in spiritual discussions provides a platform to exchange ideas and foster collective energy that uplifts everyone involved. It's a reminder that while spirituality is deeply personal, shared experiences can magnify our understanding and reinforce our commitment to spiritual paths.

Being part of a community doesn't necessarily mean large groups; even small gatherings with friends who share similar interests can have profound impacts. These discussions may highlight diverse perspectives, sparking new ways of thinking or revealing blind spots we hadn't noticed. In a community, we also find accountability partners who gently remind us of our intentions and help keep us aligned with our spiritual goals.

Each of these elements—daily rituals, connection with nature, the use of crystals and oils, and engaging with a community—works individually and collectively to fortify and sustain our spiritual growth. Together, they foster an environment where the crown chakra can thrive, leading to heightened intuition, greater self-awareness, and a deeper connection with the divine.

Final Insights

Exploring the crown chakra's role in spiritual awakening and universal connection, this chapter delved into how practices like prayer and meditation can help connect us with a higher consciousness. Through heartfelt conversations in prayer, we seek guidance and express gratitude, establishing a link to something far greater than ourselves. Meanwhile, meditation practices focused on the crown chakra allow individuals to experience heightened awareness and peace, opening doors to universal consciousness. By using visualization techniques during meditation, we engage more deeply with this sense of unity, experiencing profound sensations of connectedness.

Creating a sacred space for these activities fosters a regular practice that enriches our spiritual journeys. Whether it's a simple corner filled with calming objects or a chosen time dedicated to meditation or prayer, these elements enhance our commitment to spiritual exploration. Balancing the ego with higher consciousness through journaling, acts of service, and surrender allows us to approach life with empathy and patience, encouraging personal growth. As we embrace these practices daily—through connections with nature, using crystals and essential oils, and engaging with a supportive community—we nurture our spiritual path, allowing our crown chakra to thrive and leading to deeper self-awareness and a stronger bond with the divine.

Crown Chakra Meditation (Sahasrara)

Focus: Spiritual Connection, Higher Consciousness

Duration: 10-15 minutes

- Find a Comfortable Position: Sit with your spine straight, hands resting on your knees, palms facing upward.
- Begin Visualization: Imagine a bright, pure white or violet light radiating from the top of your head. This light connects you to universal consciousness and higher wisdom.
- Breathwork: Inhale deeply, allowing this light to flow through you, connecting you to the divine. As you exhale, release any feelings of disconnection or isolation.
- Affirmation: Repeat: "I am connected to the universe. I am one with divine energy."
- Close the Meditation: Slowly bring your attention back to your body, gently stretch, and open your eyes when you are ready.

These meditations can help balance your chakras and bring harmony to your mind, body, and spirit. You can focus on one chakra at a time or combine them for a full chakra balancing session.

Conclusion

As we close this enlightening journey through the chakras, it's a perfect moment to pause and reflect on what we've learned and how these insights can transform our lives. We've traveled from the foundational energy of the root chakra, which grounds us to the earth and gives us a sense of security, all the way up to the crown chakra, where enlightenment and spiritual connection reside. Each stop along the way has taught us about the intricate interplay between our physical selves and our emotional and spiritual well-being.

Every chapter of this book has been an opportunity to dive deep into understanding each chakra's unique qualities. The sacral chakra invited us to embrace creativity and passion, stirring within us a newfound appreciation for joy and intimacy in our lives. Then, moving upward, the solar plexus chakra powered us with confidence and determination, encouraging us to take control of our personal power and pursue our goals with tenacity.

Our heart chakra reminded us of the profound ability of love and compassion to heal and connect, not just with others but also within ourselves—teaching us to be kinder to both. Through the throat chakra, we discovered the liberating force of communication, learning that expressing our truth is essential to living authentically. The third eye chakra brought clarity and intuition into our decision-making processes, allowing us to see beyond the immediate, tapping into deeper wisdom.

And finally, as we arrived at the crown chakra, we opened ourselves to broader spiritual insights, understanding our place in the universe and the interconnectedness of all life. Realizing how these energy centers influence every aspect of our existence has been nothing short of transformative. Together, they form a system that seeks balance and harmony—a testament to their importance in nurturing our overall health.

Now that we've gathered these pearls of wisdom, the true magic begins when we apply them daily. Remember that everything you've learned isn't just theory but a toolkit for life's challenges. Integrate these practices into your routine: perhaps starting the day with a grounding meditation or pausing midday for a breath-work session that brings focus and calm. Even setting aside a few minutes before bed for chakra alignment can work wonders over time.

The beauty of these practices is their accessibility; you don't need special equipment or extensive knowledge to begin. A simple deep breath can indeed connect you to the calming energy of the solar plexus, boosting your self-assurance as you face whatever lies ahead. Experiment with these techniques and find what resonates most with you, tailoring your practice to suit your needs and lifestyle.

While this book provides a solid foundation, the world of chakras is vast and brimming with opportunities for further exploration. Consider diving deeper into specific areas that intrigue you. There are myriad resources out there—books, online courses, and guided meditations—that can enhance your understanding. Engaging with local workshops or joining online forums connects you with a community of like-minded individuals eager to share experiences and support each other's growth.

Embracing this path opens a door to continuous discovery. It's a journey without a set destination, one where every step enriches your understanding and strengthens your inner balance. So keep an open mind and stay curious, knowing that each day presents new opportunities to learn and grow.

Having a balanced chakra system significantly influences our wellness. It aligns us with a holistic perspective that champions the integration of mind, body, and spirit. In doing so, we empower ourselves—recognizing that every decision we make and every breath we take contributes to the harmony of our chakras and ultimately, the life we create.

This empowerment speaks to the core of personal transformation. You're not merely a passenger along this journey but the driver, equipped with the tools to steer towards a more balanced and fulfilled existence. By maintaining a holistic approach, you're giving yourself the reins to shape a healthier, more harmonious future.

Take these teachings with you as a guide—an anchor during turbulent times and a light illuminating the path of your personal evolution. Stay committed to nurturing your chakra health, remembering that small, consistent steps will lead to profound change. Your journey doesn't end here; it's just the beginning of a lifelong exploration of natural health and wellness.

Look forward to the discoveries yet to come, and trust in your growing ability to navigate your own path. Life's complexities become more approachable when viewed through the lens of balanced chakras. You now carry with you a deeper understanding of yourself and the energies that flow within, harnessing them to live fully and intentionally.

With these tools, may you continue to heal, grow, and explore the vibrant tapestry of life, embracing all its colors and textures. As you walk this path of self-discovery, never underestimate the power you hold—guided by the wisdom of your chakras, you have all it takes to forge a future rich with meaning and vitality.

Dear Reader,

If you have found this book useful and enjoyable, please consider leaving a review or a rating. It helps authors enormously when you do this as it gets our books seen more easily, and means we can grow our community of holistic health advocates.

Many thanks to you if you are able to do this!

sincerely,

Natasha Parker

References

1. A Powerful Mind - A Third Eye Chakra Meditation. (2024). The-Guided-Meditation-Site.com. https://www.the-guided-meditation-site.com/a-powerful-mind.html

2. Arohan Yoga. (2019, September 20). Introduction to chakras – Learn the 7 Chakras. Arohan Yoga. https://arohanyoga.com/blog/seven-chakras-in-the-body/

3. And, B. (2024). Overcoming Blocks And Limiting Beliefs Through Visualization - FasterCapital. FasterCapital. https://fastercapital.com/topics/overcoming-blocks-and-limiting-beliefs-through-visualization.html

4. Balancing Consciousness and Ego for True Fulfillment: A Spiritual Perspective. (2024). Dr. Abundant. https://

www.drabundant.com/p/balancing-consciousness-and-ego-for-true-fulfillment-a-spiritual-perspective

5. Brown, J. (2024, July 5). Unlocking the Power Within: Exploring Chakras and Meditation. Manifest Everyday. https://manifesteveryday.com/chakras-and-meditation/

6. Chakras Solar Plexus: The Ultimate Guide to Personal Power and Self-Esteem - Goddess. (2024, July 12). Goddess Women App. https://www.goddesswomenapp.com/blog/chakras-solar-plexus/

7. Compassion Gratitude - Etsy. (2020). Etsy. https://www.etsy.com/market/compassion_gratitude?ref=lp_queries_internal_bottom-13

8. Contributors, W. E. (2021, June 28). What Are Chakras? WebMD. https://www.webmd.com/balance/what-are-chakras

9. Dieffenbach, L. (2016, November 28). Sacral Chakra Balancing: Tips to Balance and Strengthen. Wellness in Harmony. https://wellnessinharmony.com/sacral-chakra-tips-balance-strengthen/

10. Dream Interpretations, Dream Symbols, Meanings | Peacefulmind.com. (2020). Peacefulmind.com. https://www.peacefulmind.com/dreams/

11. Dream Therapy, Dream Dictionary | Peacefulmind.com. (2020). Peacefulmind.com. https://www.peacefulmind.com/energy-medicine/dream-therapy/

12. Fargo, S. (2021, May 13). Boost the Relationship with yourself with 8 Self-Compassion Exercises. Mindfulness Exercises. https://mindfulnessexercises.com/8-self-compassion-exercises-to-enhance-the-relationship-you-have-with-yourself/

13. Feeling Ungrounded? Your Root Chakra May Need Some Love. (2021, October 25). Healthline. https://www.healthline.com/health/mind-body/root-chakra-healing

14. Finding Balance of Giving and Receiving in Relationships – Pam Fullerton. (2017, January 3). Pamfullerton.com. https://pamfullerton.com/giving-and-receiving-in-all-of-our-relationships/

15. flylandnetwork. (2023, July 21). Unlocking Body's Natural Energy Channels. Flyland Recovery Network | Your Guiding Light to Recovery. https://flyland.com/tapping-into-the-natural-energy-channels-of-the-body/

16. for, T. (2023, April 18). Balearic Retreats. Balearic Retreats. https://www.balearicretreats.com/blog/understanding-the-sacral-chakra-and-techniques-for-balancing-it

17. Gold, C. (2023, May 30). 6 Foods to Balance Your Root Chakra. The Balanced CEO. https://thebalancedceo.com/foods-to-balance-your-root-chakra/

18. Honesty:, E. (2024). Emotional Intelligence: Emotional Honesty: The Truth Within: Embracing Emotional Honesty - FasterCapital. FasterCapital. https://fastercapital.com/content/Emotional-Intelligence--Emotional-Honesty---The-Truth-Within--Embracing-Emotional-Honesty.html

19. How to heal your sacral chakra to up your creative juices. (2020, January 1). Well+Good. https://www.wellandgood.com/sacral-chakra-healing/

20. Jesson, A. (2021, August 27). FORGIVENESS (Heart Chakra). Vitali-Chi - Here to Heal. https://vitali-chi.co/blogs/jills-health-beauty-wellbeing-blog/forgiveness-heart-chakra?srsltid=AfmBOorLyLMTf8KsRZxjfi8fp5lo-UXisLKul8j-xZQMfsT06BKkL7qP

21. Keen Editorial Staff. (2024). Solar Plexus Affirmations: Strengthen Your Inner Power | Keen - Keen Articles. Keen.com. https://www.keen.com/articles/spiritual/solar-plexus-chakra-affirmations

22. Kloiber, R. (2024, March 23). The Throat Chakra: The Vital Center for Communication and Self-Expression. Divine

Spark. https://www.divinesparkva.com/single-post/the-throat-chakra-the-vital-center-for-communication-and-self-expression

23. Lindberg, S. (2020, September 21). Throat Chakra Healing: How to Unblock for Better Health. Healthline. https://www.healthline.com/health/throat-chakra-healing

24. Mayo Clinic Staff. (2020, May 29). Being assertive: Reduce stress, communicate better. Mayo Clinic. https://www.mayoclinic.org/healthy-lifestyle/stress-management/in-depth/assertive/art-20044644

25. meidiate. (2024). Understanding the Ego and its Desire to Sabotage your Spiritual Progress | Meditate A Center for Healing Arts. Meditatecenter.com. https://www.meditatecenter.com/understanding-the-ego-and-its-desire-to-sabotage-your-spiritual-progress/

26. Mosey, T. (2014, May 19). Chakra Nutrition - IDEA Health & Fitness Association. IDEA Health & Fitness Association. https://www.ideafit.com/chakra-nutrition/

27. OctoberCMS. (2024). Grounding Techniques for Anxiety: Balancing Muladhara. https://sattvayogaacademy.com/balancing-muladhara-grounding-techniques-anxiety-relief

28. Oducado, R. M. F. (2021, May 9). Influence of self-esteem, psychological empowerment, and empowering leader

behaviors on assertive behaviors of staff nurses. Belitung Nursing Journal. https://doi.org/10.33546/bnj.1424

29. Patrick Paul Garlinger. (2021, January 21). How to Heal Your Chakras with Forgiveness - Age of Empathy - Medium. Medium; Age of Empathy. https://medium.com/age-of-empathy/are-you-ready-to-elevate-your-chakra-healing-32a9748fcb94

30. Personal, in. (2024). Personal Development: Effective Communication: Speak Your Truth: Effective Communication in Personal Development - FasterCapital. FasterCapital. https://fastercapital.com/content/Personal-Development--Effective-Communication---Speak-Your-Truth--Effective-Communication-in-Personal-Development.html

31. Reid, R. (2023, December 24). Singing Cool Down: A Must-Have Routine for singers - Rebecca Reid - Medium. Medium. https://medium.com/@rebeccareidvocalstudio/singing-cool-down-a-must-have-routine-for-singers-f1aaa9558cfb

32. Reid, R. (2024, March). Effective Breathing and Relaxation Techniques for Anxious Singers. Medium; Medium. https://medium.com/@rebeccareidvocalstudio/effective-

breathing-and-relaxation-techniques-for-anxious-singers-fa4397adf6cc

33. Rose, E. (2020, June 6). The Art of Receiving Love - Hello, Love - Medium. Medium; Hello, Love. https://medium.com/hello-love/the-art-of-receiving-love-592c566e3d5b

34. Snyder, K. (2022, January 25). Looking for Stronger Intuition? Try This Third Eye Meditation. Yoga Journal. https://www.yogajournal.com/meditation/third-eye-meditation-for-intuition/

35. Solar, I. (2021, October 27). Spirited Earthling. Spirited Earthling. https://www.spiritedearthling.com/affirmations/7-important-solar-plexus-chakra-affirmations-for-personal-power

36. Stelter, G. (2016, October 4). A Beginner's Guide to the 7 Chakras and Their Meanings. Healthline; Healthline Media. https://www.healthline.com/health/fitness-exercise/7-chakras

37. Stokes, V. (2021, December 6). Want to Deepen Your Sensuality? Look to the Sacral Chakra. Healthline. https://www.healthline.com/health/mind-body/sacral-chakra

38. Thrive, T. T. at B. Y. B. S. and. (2023, May 25). The Science Behind Chakra Healing and Spiritual Wellness. Thrive Counseling. https://www.bybsandthrive.com/post/the-science-behind-chakra-healing-and-spiritual-wellness

39. Tremaine, L. (2014, February 11). How to Release Negative Patterns Effectively. Leightremaine.com. https://leightremaine.com/release-negative-patterns-effectively/

40. Try This Chakra Meditation to Balance Your Body's Energy System Today. (2021, February). Art of Living (United States). https://www.artofliving.org/us-en/meditation/chakras/chakra-meditation

41. Villines, Z. (2022, May 24). What are chakras? Concept, origins, and effect on health. Www.medicalnewstoday.com. https://www.medicalnewstoday.com/articles/what-are-chakras-concept-origins-and-effect-on-health

42. Warning Signs Your Chakras Are Out of Balance. (2014, November 17). Flex Studio. https://flexhk.com/blog/warning-signs-your-chakras-are-out-of-balance/

43. What is the Role of Prayer and Meditation in Connecting with God or the Universe? (2024). Earth. https://vocal.media/earth/what-is-the-role-of-prayer-and-meditation-in-connecting-with-god-or-the-universe

44. Whitney. (2020, May 25). Quickstart Guide to Balancing the Root Chakra. Moon Wandering. https://moonwandering.com/quickstart-guide-to-balancing-the-root-chakra

Printed in Great Britain
by Amazon